Maria Anne Hirschmann

WILL THE EAST WIND BLOW ?

Hansi Reports on the Middle East

S.P.A.R.C. PUBLISHING COMPANY
HUNTINGTON BEACH, CA 92648

T5-AQR-402

Scripture quotations in this publication are from the *New American Standard Bible.* © The Lockman Foundation 1960, 1962, 1963, 1968, 1971. Used by permission.

Quotations from *The Revolt*, by Menachem Begin, used by permission of Stern Matzky's Agency, Ltd., P.O. Box 628, Tel Aviv, 1952.

Poem "Peace Is Good" from *My Shalom, My Peace,*
edited by Jacob Zim. English Translation Copyright © 1975 by Sabra Books, Tel Aviv. Used with permission of the publisher, McGraw-Hill Book Company.

"No Man Is an Island" by Joan Whitney and Alex Kramer.
Copyright © 1950 by BOURNE CO. Copyright renewed. Used by permission.

© 1979 by Maria Anne Hirschmann, Hansi Ministries, Inc.
Huntington Beach, California 92648.

Published by S.P.A.R.C. Publishing Company
for Hansi Ministries, Inc.
Huntington Beach, California 92648
Printed in U.S.A.

Distributed by SPARC Publishing Company

Library of Congress Catalog Card No. 78-71319.
ISBN 0-932878-04-0

Introduction

Hansi and I packed our suitcases for a visit to the Middle East and could not help but wonder what the Lord had in store for us. One thing we knew for sure, we were going to an ancient land where jealousy and strife had been a way of life for thousands of years. My mind went back to the days of Abraham and I read again some ancient words from Genesis 21. "Now Sarah saw the son of Hagar the Egyptian, whom she had borne to Abraham, mocking. But God said to Abraham, 'Do not be distressed because of the lad and your maid; whatever Sarah tells you, listen to her, for through Isaac your descendents shall be named. And of the son of the maid I will make a nation also, because he is your descendent' " (verses 9,12,13).

We were on our way to visit those two nations: Israel descended from Isaac and Egypt the land of Ishmael. We knew there were peace talks in the news. Would we see the first break through? Or, would the wind blow from the East again and bring another storm?

We visited! We saw! We asked questions! We formed impressions! And in this book Hansi shares with you what God showed us. We are glad for the opportunity to tell both sides of the story so that you can decide for yourself, "Will the East Wind Blow?"

Betty Pershing
Huntington Beach, CA
October, 1978

January 17—Tuesday Evening

We got to the International Airport with much time to spare. I like that. I hate to rush clear up to the moment that I drop exhausted into the airplane seat, waiting for the plane to take off. We also missed the heavy Los Angeles afternoon traffic. Everything went smoothly for a change.

Betty checked both of us in while I sat and finished a few letters I hadn't been able to answer before leaving home. I wanted to mail them while still in the United States.

I wasn't sure if Betty was trying to tease me. "The flight is canceled," she said as she came back to the bench.

"Honest?" I grinned at her.

"No, it's not cancelled, we just have to be re-routed to Copenhagen instead of to London because our plane's engine blew up," Betty said matter-of-factly.

"Then we miss our connection to Geneva?" I stated just as matter-of-factly.

"Yes, but they promised to call our friends and announce the new arrival time. We'll be in Switzerland late tomorrow night."

I sighed before my heart reminded me, "Give thanks in *all* things (1 Thessalonians 5:18).

"Yes, Lord," I said. "I know you are doing it for a special reason and I thank you for it. You know best, and you are putting us on another plane to another place for our own good. It's just so much longer to Copenhagen than to London, and we'll be half dead with jet lag by the time we arrive in Geneva."

5

We had so much time to spare that Betty and I decided to eat dinner in the airport's tower restaurant to bridge our waiting hours. We had never eaten there. It was fun. The food was excellent and the view better yet. The vegetables were crunchy delicious and the waiters polite. Los Angeles glowed in orange and purple sunset colors. Jet plane after silver jet plane flew in and out below us. The planes often seemed to land and take off just one minute apart. What a busy place! What a hectic pace of life!

As our plane took off, we left many stand-by passengers behind. If we hadn't arrived so early we would have had to go first to New York and tomorrow into Europe. We would have lost twelve more hours. "Thank you, Lord!"

The plane is very full. Several families with lively children are with us in the non-smoking section. Beside Betty sits a bearded middle-aged man with several bandaged fingers. He glares at us under bushy eyebrows and hasn't cracked one small polite smile at anyone, not even the stewardess. I wonder if he even knows how to smile. What makes him so sober and sour looking? Is he afraid that two elderly ladies beside him will want to talk his ears off if he lets his scowl go? If he weren't so afraid to be human and sociable he might know the formula, "how to look happy," by the time he gets off this plane. We would love to share some good news with him—that Jesus has the answer for unhappy lives and sober-looking people anywhere, anytime, and any place!

Two young girls sit beside me, chatting together in a Scandinavian language. They must have visited the United States and are on their way home.

People fascinate me. I always try to figure out what's behind a stranger's closed-up face, what caused his deep wrinkles, the blank stare, the isolating wall he draws so eagerly around himself.

Here we are, several hundred people crowded together on a tiny flying island, floating through space and time for a short night and a long day. All of us God's children, created in His image—and culture forbids us to act like we all belong to the same human family.

We will part as we arrived—total strangers!

January 18—Wednesday Evening

Twenty-one hours ago Betty and I left by car for the Los Angeles airport. We have been "up" and going for more than a day by now. We are circling over Geneva and expect to do so for another couple of hours.

The aircraft cannot land due to heavy snowfall. That's unusual for Geneva. They must have had a bad storm from the north. The captain announced that runways are being cleared but if landing is not possible within two more hours we'll be sent to an alternate airport. The plane has only two hours of fuel left. As we listened to the announcement Betty said, "Okay, Lord!" I nodded. We both are, by now, pretty eager for a hot shower and a bed.

We dozed fitfully a few hours across the Atlantic. The plane was too full to stretch out. I had never flown over the North Pole in winter before and I wasn't

7

prepared for the long night and the short day. Traveling in the summertime we always fly into the midnight sun and usually have breakfast over the Atlantic shortly after my watch shows that it is midnight in California. This time, in January, morning dawn came later and by the time we finished breakfast, dusk began to settle for a night landing in Copenhagen.

Where had eight hours of daylight gone? Betty and I puzzled over it until I remembered that our flight route went over the Arctic Circle, which has hardly any sunlight for endless winter weeks.

We landed late in Copenhagen due to heavy head winds. Most of the passengers were enroute to London. Just as we got ready to find our gate to connect for Geneva, we heard the announcement that flights to London were cancelled due to fog and bad weather. Betty and I looked at each other, "Thank You, Lord," I said gratefully, "for re-routing us and keeping us out of London. We would never have gotten out if we had landed there. And it's no fun to be in London in the fog!"

So, now we are circling over Geneva with several other planes in the same holding pattern. Where will we end up? Milan? Rome? Florence? Or even Zurich? Betty hopes it might be her favorite place, Interlaken. God has a way of surprising us and we can trust Him!

The stewardesses try to keep the passengers happy by serving drinks. Most seats are occupied by men—obviously businessmen—who speak French. The talking and laughing gets louder and louder as more liquor flows. We sit quietly and look out into the night. We are flying above the clouds and a bright moon shines down on us.

I wonder if Mister Bushy Eyebrows made his connection to Munich after he left us in Copenhagen. He finally broke down and exchanged a few sentences with Betty. He even smiled faintly once after he had his first cup of morning coffee and we got ready to land. He told her that he was on his way to Germany. He never permitted himself or us to become acquainted with each other beyond those few words. Too bad! I wanted to talk to him. I also wanted to see him smile big. I still wonder if he knows how. People's faces change so surprisingly when they smile. The homeliest face turns pretty with a big smile. Why don't people use that beautifier more, rather than alcohol, to loosen faces and personalities?

In front of us sits a middle-aged businessman who is getting obviously more and more drunk. I don't understand his French but Betty figured out that he is bugging the stewardess to call Washington, D.C. immediately—from the air! The others around him laugh. Why is it so easy to laugh together about other people's foolishness when intoxicated but stay distant and sober when being "just normal"?

Whenever I find myself alone in a crowd, I think of one of my favorite songs: "No Man Is an Island"!

> *No man is an island.*
> *No man stands alone,*
> *Each man's joy is joy to me.*
> *Each man's grief is my own.*
> *We need one another*
> *So I will defend*
> *Each man as my brother,*
> *Each man as my friend.*

9

January 20—Friday Night

It is exciting to live in a time of modern technology that can bring a person from a snowstorm to a sandstorm in a matter of hours.

We landed Wednesday night, after two weary hours of circling Geneva, and fell into a hotel bed by midnight. It was too late to call my friend, Margie, and so we stayed near the airport overnight.

We Americans are spoiled! I couldn't believe that the hotel would have no limousine to pick us up. We had to stand in a long line waiting for a taxi and we watched people cut in.

When we finally got our turn, the taxi driver pointed at our two luggage pieces and then at his Toyota and shook his head. We don't speak French but I understood. His trunk was too small for our suitcases. To think that Betty and I had been *so* proud because we traveled *so* light. Only two suitcases for two American women for a three-week tour!

My feelings were deeply hurt! A bigger taxi finally gave us a ride, overcharged us, of course (because we were rich Americans). Then we dragged our "light" luggage by ourselves up the stairs because no porter was available.

Enough hot water came out of the pipe to get a quick rinse off. I felt so exhausted I knew I could sleep for the next twenty-four hours. However, four hours later I awoke and looked at my watch which still carried California time. It was 7 P.M.—and I was wide awake!

By 8:00 A.M., Geneva time, I called Margie. She

picked us up at noon. By then I felt sleepy again, but I decided to fight it through without a nap. We find that jet lag is best cured by forcing our bodies to stay awake until they adjust.

The snowstorm left a winter wonderland behind. We feasted our eyes on the beauty of sunny snow-glistening mountains under a deep blue sky—and *froze*. California blood is thin, at least mine is! So I shivered through the day while we visited several Swiss friends. They all nursed us along with warm friendship and cups of hot tea.

This morning we flew first into Rome and then to Cairo. I don't like to fly the Italian airlines. They don't treat women very politely. Rome seems to be the dividing line between Western and Eastern culture. It's in Rome where I usually get my first rude pushes and shoves. Some of the men always try to be first in line, though they sit on the benches to the very last moment before boarding.

Betty and I always try to get near the boarding area when the plane has open seating so that we can scramble for the non-smoking area. The Eastern male gets rather annoyed that a Western woman will not budge when he pushes her away with his elbow. Well, if I have stood patiently and sometimes rather endlessly near the gate, I don't step aside. I wear my little American flag on my lapel and act like I don't know that the women of the Eastern culture are expected to bow to *any* male.

We ended up in the non-smoking section as planned. I watched a man beside us light up his very strong cigarette as soon as the plane took off. I tapped the gentleman on his shoulder and pointed to the non-

11

smoking sign. He was so flabbergasted by my bold behavior he didn't smoke for the rest of the flight.

As we approached Cairo we could hear the sand beat against the cabin window of our aircraft. We looked into a yellow haze down below.

"Egypt welcomes us with a sandstorm," Betty smiled. "I hope it stops long enough so we can see the pyramids and the sphinx without getting our eyes full of sand." She had been in Egypt before and looked searchingly out the window. "I hope we can see the pyramids from the air, it's a great way to begin a visit to Egypt!"

I blinked in a daze. I don't think very clearly while in the last pangs of jet lag and with a groggy headache. "I am going to see the pyramids," I said and came suddenly alive. "Betty," I felt overwhelmed, "I, the little orphan girl from Czechoslovakia, who grew up in a small mountain village and slept in a hayloft, am actually visiting the land of the Pharaohs and the sphinx!"

"Not only that," Betty nodded and smiled big, "but you are coming here to meet the leaders of the land, maybe even the president. You have come a long way!"

The plane began to descend. I gazed below me through our sand-scratched plane window into a vast ocean of yellow waves of sand. As far as my eyes could see was desert, uninhabited, endless desert, land without a sign of life or vegetation.

"Is this Egypt?" I thought. "The land of the Old Testament my foster mother read to me about when I was a little girl? Is this the land the children of Israel left in ancient times? Is this the place they demanded to come back to when the going was rough in the exodus to Canaan? How can anyone live in such a wasteland?"

Betty seemed to have guessed my thoughts. "What you see is part of the Sahara Desert. Nothing grows down there, not even cactus or small bushes. It's not like the California desert," she smiled again. "It's nothing but sand: fine, crystal-sharp, cutting, hot sand."

"Is all of Egypt sand?" I asked. "How can people exist in such a place?"

"Watch as we approach," she said, "through the desert winds for a small strip of green land. It is the Nile Valley. That is where most of the people live. At the edges of the green land you may find bedouins in some oases. But wherever the water ends, life ends! The Nile is the giver of life for Egypt. Without it the land would die."

The plane dipped toward landing and my ears popped. Just then the first small strip of green land appeared. "Over there are the pyramids," Betty pointed toward the west. Beside the small green band of life, amidst the yellow waves of the rigid sea of dead sand, I watched as three monuments grew taller and clearer and disappeared again into the haze. I shook my head in disbelief.

"Did I really just see the great tombs of the Pharaohs," I said, "or am I dreaming?"

"No, you just were welcomed by the same ancient pyramids that greeted Abraham when he came to Egypt. They were *very* old already when he arrived," Betty informed me patiently. She obviously enjoyed my rising excitement and I felt so grateful that she was

13

by my side. She knows so much about the history—past and present—of the entire Middle East and shares so willingly and without an air of superiority.

The plane lowered its landing gear and the loud speaker told us to fasten our seat belts and put the back of our seats into upright position. "Here we come," Betty sighed. "I hope your Egyptian friend is at the airport. The Cairo airport and Egyptian customs can be absolute misery and endless hours of waiting."

The wheels touched for a rough landing and we found ourselves in a cloud of dust, sand, noise and strangers.

January 21—
Early Saturday Morning

As we started down the wobbly steps from the plane to the ground, sand stung our faces like needles. The desert wind tossed papers, garbage and other loose stuff around.

"Betty, Cairo reminds me of airports in the far East," I said. "It has that kind of a primitive look in spite of the size and the big buildings."

Betty nodded. "Don't let the primitive look deceive you," she said soberly. "They make up for it inside with red tape and complicated custom regulations. Brace yourself for hours of hassle and waiting—unless your Egyptian friend has some pull."

I shrugged my shoulders. I didn't know what to expect. The whole idea for this trip had come without any planning on our part in the first place. I was speaking at an international Christian Endeavor youth convention in Pennsylvania last summer while receiving a special award. Young people from many countries were present. After the meeting a dark-haired, short, middle-aged gentleman approached me and said, "Hansi, when will you come and visit us in Egypt?" He introduced himself as a Christian Egyptian businessman who had come to the United States for some special business conventions. He also had brought an Egyptian youth delegation to the Christian congress. He attended the congress between business sessions.

I said, "I never gave any thought of going to Egypt. I figure God will show me if I ever should do so."

Mr. Hermina urged me to pray about it and ended by saying, "If you come, I will introduce you to President Sadat."

I laughed and said, "If you do that I might have to write a book about the Middle East!"

I did pray about it and as a result Betty and I are now in Cairo and hopefully, in the following weeks, in Jordan and Israel, too.

"I wonder if anyone will be here to meet us," I sighed. The place looked crowded and I questioned if I even would recognize the man again if he was here. A few pangs of panic hit me. The language we listened to had no similarity to English or German, the only two tongues I understand. We had no idea which hotel had reservations for us because our Egyptian friend had told us that he would make all the arrangements. What if we missed each other?

My fears proved ungrounded. As we entered the

building, I saw his broad smiling face. He welcomed us most graciously and introduced us to a young Egyptian gentleman and a young lady, both in Western clothing.

I didn't catch the titles and descriptions but I understood that it had something to do with the government. Both were there to help us—and help they did.

We were ushered past long waiting lines into a room with overstuffed furniture and the smell of cigars and Turkish coffee—the VIP room!

"President Sadat received Prime Minister Begin here," Mr. Hermina said. "Please make yourselves at home."

"If you hand us your passports and luggage tags, we shall take care of everything," the young man said politely.

Betty gave him what he asked for and we sat down to wait and chat with Mr. Hermina's wife and two teenage daughters who had come to welcome us, too.

We had visited for an hour or a bit longer when the two young government guides reappeared and told us that everything had been cleared and our luggage was loaded in the limousine.

As we walked out to get into the car, Betty motioned with her eyes toward the crowds. Most of the passengers of our flight were still in line to have their passports cleared. Nobody had entered the custom checkpoints yet. "God is good to us," she murmured. "Whoever your Egyptian friend is, he knows how to pull strings in our favor."

"Please, be assured that we will do everything to make your visit in Egypt pleasant and worth your

16

while," Mr. Hermina said. "Consider yourselves guests of the president and our government. We are at your disposal and if you tell us what you want to see or do, we shall arrange it."

"Right now we would like to go to our hotel, unpack and get a hot meal," Betty said pleasantly, but rather firmly. "Hansi shouldn't have too many activities until she has had a good night's sleep. We are still not over the jet lag."

I gave her a grateful look. One problem of being treated as a celebrity is the fact that so many people are too kind. They try too hard to help or please and I end up over-scheduled, over-fed, over-tired. Whoever travels with me has to run interference for me.

So, to the hotel we went for dinner with the Hermina family and early retirement for the night. We stayed in the Shepherd's Hotel which pleased Betty.

"It has an Egyptian flavor and will give you the 'feel' of the oriental culture a lot more than the Hilton or some of the Western hotels," Betty said quietly.

Several doorkeepers in bright red Turkish trousers, with gold-braided epaulets on their shoulders greeted us. They looked like characters out of the Arabian Nights. I wondered what was said since nobody held his hand out to us for a tip. They did so to everybody else.

Our room was on the seventh floor and the night view from our balcony took my breath away. Below us flowed the dark waters of the Nile reflecting like a mirror every light of its surroundings—the lit-up tower of Cairo, some color-blazing nightclubs, and several high-rise buildings. Only once had I seen such a magnificent display of light reflections before—when I

17

looked at Lake Geneva in Switzerland one clear evening after the rains had stopped. The night view of the Nile topped anything I had seen before, and Betty looked surprised too. "I cannot remember that I ever saw this kind of a night scene before on my previous visits," she said. "The Nile looks as clear as glass!"

We ate in an ornate, overly-decorated dining room. The place swarmed with waiters, head waiters, servant girls and youngsters who were obviously trainees for future service jobs. I observed a certain pecking order in the color of their uniforms or outfits. The headman wore a golden blazer—Western type. All he did was snap his fingers and give orders while he wandered around the dining room. He never did any manual work—neither did the fellow who took our orders. He wrote down what we had chosen and handed the paper to another waiter who passed it on to the kitchen.

Each rank wore a different-colored blazer. The lowest in order were obviously the men in Egyptian garb—a nightgown-like, long robe in various colors, called a *galabia,* and a head cover called a *kaffia.* The kaffia was a white square piece of cloth. The front edge covered the forehead, a ropelike ring in black held it in place around the head. The other corners were draped over the shoulders. These servants served us the meals and water or tea.

Mr. Hermina must have known from previous experiences that Westerners don't drink Egyptian water. He ordered a bottle of mineral water before we requested it. We were glad. Betty had warned me that, while we were in Egypt or Jordan, under no circumstances whatsoever could we drink unboiled water or eat any raw vegetables or fruit unless we could peel it ourselves. The only safe liquids were wine, coffee, tea or bottled drinks. Since we didn't use coffee or wine, we didn't have too many choices left.

The mineral water we drank had been bottled in West Germany and proved to be uncarbonated. "Good," Betty sighed and continued under her breath, "that will make brushing our teeth less complicated. It's misery to brush teeth with carbonated water. The toothpaste foams out of your mouth."

We both giggled and the Herminas looked puzzled. No questions. They looked more puzzled when we declined the most delicious looking salad plate of fresh crisp greens and tomatoes.

"No salad for either of you?" Mrs. Hermina asked. "It's good for you!"

I nodded. I knew that fresh salads were important to a balanced diet and I would miss salads most for the next ten days. I lived on such stuff back home. But I knew also that the Egyptians water their fields with recycled, unpurified water, the same water they drink and bathe in. Egypt for the most part has no sewage system. All human and other wastes spill into the Nile and canal waters and pollute them dangerously. I had faced the same problem before while traveling in Mexico and managed not to get sick. I was determined to stay well for the entire Middle East tour and not get the famous "Middle East runs" either.

I tried to be polite. The natives of a land obviously develop an immunity to those bugs which we Westerners don't have. I smiled at our hosts, "Sometimes salad makes me sick," I said, "as I have a sensitive stomach." Betty grinned again.

We asked for fruit in place of dessert and got some tangerines, oranges and thin reddish bananas. We peeled the fruit carefully and enjoyed the taste of tree-ripened sweetness in them, something we seldom get in America.

When we finally retired to our rooms, Betty said to our host, "We surely would like to see the pyramids tomorrow and attend the Sound and Light program in the evening—if that is agreeable with you."

Mr. Hermina nodded eagerly. "Whatever you wish shall be done. If the winds stop we can go. If the sandstorm blows from the west like today, we will not be able to go to the desert. We must wait and see!" We said good night to each other and took the elevator to our room.

I walked out to our balcony, looked up into the star-studded night sky and said, "Please, God, stop the winds. You wouldn't bring me to Egypt and not let me see the pyramids and the sphinx. You wouldn't do *that* to me, I know for sure, and I thank you for it already."

Then, I got ready to take my shower and Betty reminded me to keep my eyes and mouth closed while showering. She also warned me *not* to pull on a cord that hung down from the wall. "They tell me that someone appears at your door to wash your back if you pull this string," she said, "and it's the opposite sex—a young boy for the ladies, a young girl for the men."

I didn't think I needed that kind of service. I remembered also to brush my teeth with mineral water—then opened the faucet to rinse my brush!

"Oh, dear," I called to Betty, "I forgot already not to use the faucet water. How will I survive ten days of it?

What do I do now, I brought only one toothbrush?"

We fished around in our toilet articles until I found some cologne that contained alcohol. I poured some of it over my toothbrush.

"If you think it is funny to foam with carbonated water out of your mouth, try the combination of cologne and toothpaste next," I said solemnly to Betty while I crawled under my covers. "It's an exotic taste!"

We laughed ourselves to sleep.

January 21— Late Saturday Evening

Tonight I saw the pyramids and temples outlined in deep blue light against a black star-studded sky in the desert. A booming low voice spoke in Oxford English over the loud speakers: "You have come tonight to the most fabulous and celebrated place in the world. Here, on the plateau of Giza, stands forever the mightiest of human achievements. No traveler, emperor, merchant or poet has trodden on these sands and not gasped in awe."

Then the face of the sphinx appeared out of the darkness, lit up gently like the golden light of dawn. Another male voice spoke: "With each new dawn I see the sun-god rise on the far bank of the Nile. . . . For five thousand years I have seen all the suns man can remember come up in the sky. I saw the history of Egypt in its first glow, as tomorrow I shall see the east burning with a new flame."

I reached under my heavy blanket for Betty's arm to pinch it. I needed to pinch somebody, either me or her, to make sure I wasn't dreaming.

I wasn't! I had never been more wide awake, shivering a bit under a scratchy wool blanket in the chilly desert air, and filled with deep wonderment. "Who am I, to sit beneath the famous pyramids and watch such a spectacle?" I whispered into Betty's ear.

"I feel the same way everytime I come here," she whispered back. "The pyramids are one of the seven wonders of the ancient world that still remain. To think that we were lucky enough to come tonight and see and hear the English version of the show!"

We not only had come for the right language presentation (the other three nights it is presented in either French, German or Arabic), we had been most politely ushered through the crowds to the first row, reserved for VIPs and were given some heavy blankets to wrap ourselves in.

I had seen one Sound and Light program two years before in Israel, at Herod's citadel in Jerusalem. I knew that many such programs existed in different countries, from the "Son et Lumiere" at Versailles to many other historic places all over the world. But to sit before a mile-and-a-quarter-long, half-mile-deep stage, created by nature and an ancient civilization and soak in the sounds and illuminations of modern times can become overwhelming to someone like me. I didn't learn much about Egyptology and ancient history in the one-room school of my childhood, neither did I dare to dream on my straw bed in the hayloft where I slept as a child that I ever would travel to such famous places.

The visit to the pyramids in the morning had been exciting enough. I rode a camel, the first one in my life. I even climbed behind an old Arab guide to the middle of the pyramid of Cheops into the royal burial chamber. I got kind of short-winded doing so. The Cheops pyramid is the largest of the three and we climbed more than 225 feet straight up. The burial place, we were told, is exactly in the middle and the tomb is built on the exact axis of north, south, east and west. I wondered how the burial room could be filled with fresh clean desert air when we finally arrived, huffing and puffing. I asked the guide.

"Ancient air conditioning," he said with a toothless grin in his parchment-wrinkled face. "The dead needed air to live again."

"It's more than that," Betty informed me quietly. "The ancient Egyptians believed that the human spirit lived in the mummy and could come out through the nose to leave the tomb and wander and roam the land. So every famous tomb has some hidden openings to the outside, otherwise the spirit would have been trapped."

The pyramids are most impressive by day, but become overwhelming and eerie when bathed in different-colored lights by night. The narrator's voice told the unbelievable story of how they were built.

"Stone by stone it was built from earth to heaven. Each pyramid was built in a Pharaoh's lifetime by one hundred thousand workmen, united in a mighty surge of faith. Each stone averages two-and-one-half tons in weight, three million blocks were hoisted up and laid one upon the other. The finest ones, of pure granite, were dug from the quarries of Aswan, whence they

The Sphinx in front of the pyramid of Cheops.

Opening to the royal tomb in the pyramid of Cheops.

came by boat carried by the flooding of the Nile."

I bent over to Betty's ear, "Aren't we visiting Aswan within the next few days?" I asked. I always have a hard time remembering names and schedules, especially in strange surroundings.

"Yes, we'll fly into Aswan on Tuesday," Betty answered, "and we'll see those quarries, including an unfinished obelisk."

The second narrator came on, after the first voice finished by saying: "These stones were hauled singly onto earth-mounds, banked higher and higher as the edifice grew."

The other voice answered: "In front of such superhuman effort can one believe in the legend of the whip? It needs mystical fervor to build a pyramid! Faith! Those who worked here deserve not our pity but our deepest respect and admiration. They lived through one of those rare times when man knows with absolute certainty what he has to do and where he has to go, because he believes. Here, man thought that death was vanquished."

The last sentences lodged into my mind: "Here, man *thought* that death was vanquished."

The sentence haunted me while I listened to the rest of the program and watched the spectacle of voices, music, sound effects and light (which in turn created unusual shade effects) take place. I took it all in, that immense city of the dead. In the foreground are the ruins of two temples and the sphinx. Behind the big pyramids are three small pyramids of queens, only recently recovered from the sand. For forty-five minutes the ancient world comes alive for us—not only in words but in other sounds, too: the games that precede

25

the choosing and consecration of the Pharaoh; the galloping of horses; the swish of flying arrows; the singing of the choirs.

Then the Pharaoh is dead and strange funeral lamentations evoke a sense of deep sadness. One follows, in vivid imagination, the funeral cortege from the temple in the valley where the funeral rites take place to the temple on the heights where the ancient priests chant the final farewell. An immense stone is released after the mummy is placed into the inner burial chamber. It rolls down on its own, closing the entrance to the pyramid from the inside. Nobody must ever enter the resting place of the carefully-prepared mummy, neither friend, foe nor grave robbers. The spirit must not be disturbed.

The final words come from the sphinx while lights flood the place in a triumphant climax: "In the course of time only human achievements crumble and fall, but the spirit which conceived these monuments cannot perish."

I sit dazed and watch the glorious scene fade slowly back into a pitch-dark night. Everyone gets up and leaves. I smile in kind gratitude as we hand back the blankets and shake hands but I cannot talk.

One sentence goes around and around in my heart and mind: "Here, man *thought* that death was vanquished."

January 22—Sunday Night

Another full day, but we found at least a few moments to glance into an American newspaper to find out what was going on in the world. I am not so sure that we will be able to meet President Anwar Sadat at the present time. The man is rather busy according to the news.

I never dreamed when first contacts for our Middle East trip were made last August, that we would arrive in Egypt just at a time when Sadat would be front-page news. The peace negotiations between Israel and Egypt had begun before we left home and things looked hopeful. Now Sadat has called his delegation abruptly back from Jerusalem and broken off the peace talks.

Last night he addressed his parliament in a very long speech. Our driver listened to it the whole evening by car radio while we were at the Sound and Light program. I wished I could understand Arabic. This morning the speech was rebroadcast, tonight it was played again. The Egyptians seem to listen and re-listen. Wherever we went, loud speakers and radios carried the speech to the people. I can sense a general excitement and agitation among the population.

I asked Mr. Hermina when he came to take us to church, what the president said and how the people felt about it.

"Sadat wants peace but the Jews want to hold on to a piece of land that is nothing but sand and dust. They are not interested in peace, they are as stubborn and obstinate as always. The Jews are troublemakers who even gave Moses and God nothing but trouble when they wandered through the wilderness for forty years."

I kept quiet. "What did Sadat say in his speech?" I asked again.

"That world opinion and America will *see* who wants peace," he said, rather agitated, "and that will force Israel to come to terms with us!"

He raved on as we walked a few blocks to church. Parking is next to impossible in certain areas of Cairo and I observed and listened as we hurried along. We were already late.

"Look at our streets," our host pointed to the ground. "They are torn open for repair and then left undone because there is no money to fix them," he said with a big frown.

We climbed over rough surface, pushed and thronged by the crowd. From the looks of it, only peasants and bazaar-keepers walk, but Cairo seems to have millions of peasants. The better class of Cairo was obviously on wheels, either by car, motorcycle, bicycle or donkey-pulled cart. A few horses and buggies mixed into the overcrowded streets also and each vehicle demanded passage—the car drivers honked without end and animal drivers yelled and threatened. Pedestrians had to watch carefully. Nobody on wheels was willing to stop for someone on foot—we had to jump aside fast on several occasions when vehicles passed each other in the small side streets. Across the streets hung many colorful banners carrying oversized pictures of Sadat—the writings were often not only in Arabic but also in English. "We back you up in your cause, President Sadat," one sign read. "We know you are right."

"We will have peace through President Sadat," another huge sign read while the smiling face of Sadat looked benevolently down upon the masses.

"Betty, something bothers me about this whole thing," I said softly before we entered through a high iron gate into the quietness of the church. "I am feeling something in the air of this land that disturbs me greatly. I can't put my finger on it, but it's something I have seen before in my life and it's not good!"

The large Presbyterian church was only sparsely filled. They had a guest speaker from America who had come directly from a preacher's seminar for Christian ministers in the Cairo area. I was asked to speak to the people for a couple of minutes, since I had been invited to conduct the Sunday evening meeting. The young minister interpreted for both of us Americans. I had no idea what he said and I received no feedback from the audience. The people sat in stoic silence and never moved a muscle. I wondered if smiling was forbidden during the worship service, for the people smiled at us when the service was finally over. Several church members welcomed us and told me that they looked forward to the evening service.

During lunch with our host I began to ask questions again. "Do you have freedom of worship in Egypt?" I asked Mr. Hermina. (Our government guide wasn't due until later, so I dared to ask our friend about some sensitive issues.)

"We don't have the freedom you have in America," he said in a low voice, "but things are so much better since Sadat took over. We are not allowed to do any mission work in public, but we are permitted to have services. Under Nasser it was much harder. He kicked out all the foreign missionaries who had come to help us! None of them have had permission yet to return."

"How many Christians are there in Egypt? Have the missionaries brought Christianity to this Moslem country just recently?"

My host acted offended. "The Coptic Church has existed in this part of the world long before the Moslems came," he said defensively. "When the Moslems conquered this land they turned Coptic churches into mosques. We trace the beginnings of the Coptic Church to the time of Christ. When the Moslems overran the Middle East, nearly seven hundred years after the birth of Christ, they forced the common people to accept Mohammed's teachings." He stretched his wrist toward us. "The custom to have a cross tattooed to the wrist began at that time." I had noticed the blue tatoo on his forearm before but had not paid any attention to it.

"The Christians of ancient time had a choice. They either paid a huge sum to the Moslem emperor as ransom to stay Christians or became Moslems—otherwise they had to die," he explained. "Those who were able to pay were marked with a cross. Through the generations, Christians have kept the tradition as a sign of loyalty. We are few, very few, but we are proud of our heritage." He turned to a young waitress and said something in Arabic. Shyly she stretched her wrist out toward us. A little blue cross was tattooed on her right wrist.

"She is only seventeen years old and a student at Cairo University," our host said. "Christians have to work much harder in our land to be successful. They don't get a lot of help and have a harder time finding jobs. You will find most Christians better educated than the average person in Egypt. But even with better education they get lesser pay than a Moslem."

"Does your President Sadat agree with such injustice?" I asked. "He claims that he is giving Egypt freedom and is making it a democracy."

"President Sadat is a devout Moslem himself and will always put his religion above anything else. He encourages the Moslems here in Egypt to win other people to their religion. Moslems can have any kind of program, set up tents for a street meeting, and do many things we Christians are not allowed to do," Mr. Hermina said quietly.

Our guide arrived and we walked out to the car. The driver was a small white-haired man who always wore a heavy western-style overcoat. He also carried with him at all times a string of beads with a tassel. When he drove, he hung the beads on his rear view mirror. When he left the car, he carried them with him.

"Those are worry beads," Betty said quietly when nobody was near us. "Almost every Moslem carries them and lets them slide through his fingers whenever possible. The string has thirty-three beads, for the thirty-three years of Christ's life."

"Do the Moslems believe in Christ?" I said completely surprised.

"Yes, they do, but they don't believe that He is the only Son of God. He is a prophet who lived without sin. Mohammed is the greater prophet of Allah, though he did sin!"

Our host and the guide seemed to have an argument. We couldn't understand because they spoke in

31

Arabic. They always did so and it never seemed to dawn on them that it would bother us at any time.

We never found out what the disagreement was all about until that evening when our host escorted us to the meeting where I was to speak.

"I am sorry I could not show you the Coptic Museum this afternoon," he said disgruntled, "but the guide insisted that you *must* see the Islamic Museum. He is a Moslem and very proud of the place!"

I wondered why we were taken to that museum. We had never requested it. He also took us to the Alabaster Mosque and to King Farouk's tomb. All were Moslem places.

I also had wondered why all those places were open and why we watched school children go to school on Sunday. "How come all your public buildings are open today?" I asked.

"The Moslem holiday is Friday. That's when schools and public places close down," I was told.

Oh, blissful Western ignorance which thinks that the whole wide world lives as we do. My naiveté is obviously topped only by my ability to put my foot in my mouth at the wrong moment.

I wasn't so sure that my host was too pleased with the message I gave in the Sunday evening service. The meeting was well attended. The women sat on the left side, the men on the right. Everyone was dressed in simple, mostly dark Western clothing. None wore the native costume, which was obviously Moslem garb.

I spoke through an interpreter. That is always hard work because audience feedback arrives delayed and it is difficult to establish rapport.

The Lord and I managed to get through anyway. I

32

told the people about my past and my great struggle with hate, bitterness and unforgiveness before I found Christ. "The key to healing for individuals, the church and a country is forgiveness." I said. "God has told us to pray for one another and for our enemies. That means that you as Christians have an obligation, not only to pray for your president and the peace attempts, but to pray for the Jews, too!"

I didn't look at my host while I said it. He had said many hard words about Israel since we had met at the Cairo airport and I wondered how a born-again Christian could be so harsh against anyone. And wasn't Jesus Christ a Jew?

After the interpreter translated my remarks, I watched many heads begin to nod. By the end of the meeting I saw some tears roll. One woman who sat beside Betty said, "Nobody around here preaches like her—but she is right and it is the message of the Bible!"

I couldn't stay and visit with the believers. We had a late evening appointment to meet a TV controller. He wanted to make arrangements for an international television program for the latter part of the week. So I quickly shook some out-stretched hands and we hurried back to the hotel.

The taping of the program was set for Thursday night at 10:00 P.M. I wondered how I could stay awake so late since I still struggled with the time change. But I trusted that I would do better as the days went by.

When we finally got to our room, Betty said, "I better set the alarm clock. We have awakened so far between three and four every morning. But who knows we might oversleep tomorrow morning."

33

"We better not," I said and laughed. "We cannot miss the only plane to Luxor! And who but the Egyptians would put an only flight at such an un-earthly hour—6:30 A.M. The driver will be at the entrance at 5:30—so we better sleep fast!"

January 23—Monday Evening

I woke up at four o'clock this morning and saw Betty sitting up, looking out the big window. "Look at that full moon," she said. "It's the loveliest night." We both walked barefooted out to the balcony and gasped. The silvery moon had fallen into the dark river bottom of the Nile and shimmered like an oversized pure sterling coin from the depth of the waters. Betty went for her camera and tried to capture the fairy-tale beauty of the moment, though she knew that cameras don't see as well as the human eye does. After that we just stood and tried to imprint the gorgeous picture into the storehouse of our memory until I remembered that my feet were cold and we had to get ready for the airport.

The driver was waiting when we got down to the hotel entrance—with overcoat, worry beads and a friendly smile. We like the man and he obviously likes us. What a pity we can't talk to him. I wonder if he understands any English at all. He never tries a single word of it with us.

The streets of Cairo looked strangely empty so early in the morning; the bazaars closed and deserted. I was told that Arabs begin the day at sunrise and close down at sunset. We were still in the grip of night, not even the dawn had come. It was hard to picture the streets crowded within another hour with the strangest mixtures of vehicles and people I had ever seen. Women would walk the sidewalks with heavy loads on their heads and with veils covering part of their faces. While others, mostly young females, in Western clothing and extremely high heels, would totter cautiously amidst the rubbish and loose rocks of the street.

The modern girls are not the only ones who wear high-heeled shoes in Cairo. Most young Egyptian men who dress in Western outfits wear unusually high-heeled-and-soled shoes. Our guide always wore shoes that made him at least two or three inches taller. I tried to figure out how they could possibly walk in such monstrosities, but they all manage.

Our guide was not traveling with us, only Mr. Hermina. We picked him up on the way to the airport and arrived much too early. So we sat and watched people. Finally we went through a relaxed checking of our luggage and boarded with two tour groups, one from Austria and the other from France.

We caught on fast that, without our guide, we were only normal tourists with no red-carpet treatment when we arrived at Luxor. Luckily, we didn't have to go by bus. A rickety taxi took us to the Valley of the Kings, the graveyard of the Pharaohs. We had a local guide who spoke pretty good English and knew the history of the land. He had gone to the University of Cairo and studied archaeology and he enjoyed sharing details if the tourists showed an interest. We did!

It is believed that Tuthmosis I was the Pharaoh who started what became through the centuries a honeycomb of man-made caves where monarchs were buried in secrecy.

Less than two thousand years before Christ, it was well-known that even the strongest pyramids could not protect the royal mummies and their rich provisions from greedy thieves. Tuthmosis wanted his body buried securely. He believed that only if he wasn't disturbed, could his *ka*, or spiritual form, find him and lead him safely across the river of death to the joyous life of the afterworld. He had to find a secret burial ground and he sent his favorite architect, Ineni, to find it. The monarch's faithful servant did find the perfect place in a valley five miles west of the Nile.

All ancient burial places of Egypt lie to the west of the Nile in the desert, where every evening the sun dies. East of the Nile is the side of rebirth and everlasting life, for there the sun is reborn every morning out of the darkness.

In the desolate hills of that valley, Ineni found a perfect place for his king. "I attended to the excavation of the cliff-tomb of his Majesty alone," the architect wrote in hieroglyphs on the walls of his own tomb, which is near that of Tuthmosis, "no one seeing, no one hearing."

Tuthmosis' grave was robbed after all, but it didn't stop the following Pharaohs of many centuries from burying themselves in the same valley. It is believed that no other spot on earth has held greater wealth and riches than the place called, in modern times, the Valley of the Kings. All the treasures are gone today. Greed found most of them.

Of the many graves we were able to visit, two fascinated me the most. The tomb of Seti I had my special interest. Many Bible scholars believe that he was the Pharaoh who "knew not Joseph" and made the children of Israel slaves. His grave was designed on a grand scale. It is cut into the living rock to a depth of three hundred feet and consists of six rooms. We have every reason to believe that every room was filled with treasures when he was buried in an alabaster sarcophagus.

Inscriptions on the walls and other historic evidence suggest that more than forty thousand slaves worked for more than twenty years to ready the tomb for this famous king. The dead Pharaohs demanded great things in ancient Egypt. No royal palaces of those times have survived the thousands of years, but tombs and temples have. The Pharaohs were determined to live forever and not have their memory erased.

Seti took great pains to protect his mummy. He had special provisions set aside to aid him in the afterlife. A trap, more than fifty feet deep, was dug before the inner rooms, so thieves would fall to their death. False doors and dead-end passages were designed to mislead the robbers. But it did not help. Thieves stole everything.

When Belzoni discovered the tomb in 1817, the rooms were empty and the sarcophagus without the mummy. Priests had obviously removed the body to protect the royal dead and the mummy was later found in the famous mass tomb at Deir el Bahari. Now the mummy can be seen in the Cairo Museum.

On the walls of the six burial rooms, Seti told the story of his life and death in pictures and hieroglyphs. Our guide was able to read much of it to us, but the pictures alone told a poignant story. Seti, the strong

Entrance to the tomb of Seti I.

Rooms inside Seti's tomb.

monarch who boasted of many battles and victories, was afraid of death and darkness. Thousands of stars and hundreds of sun disks, many of them carried by gods, decorate the top and sides of his final resting place. Afterlife is depicted by scenes where the gods hand the royal visitor the *ankh*, the key of life.

It was the form of the ankh that fascinated me deeply. It is a cross with a circle on top of it. The circle, to me, symbolizes divinity. "Where have I seen this sign before?" I asked Betty in a quiet moment while we stood and looked.

"The occult in America is using this sign more and more. Many young people wear it on rings and chains," she said.

"It's incredible that the sign of the cross would appear nearly two thousand years before the death of Christ," I said. "How sad it is that this Pharaoh could have looked by faith forward to life everlasting under this symbol. If he had only been willing to listen to the story his Jewish slaves knew so well—the story of a coming Messiah! Instead he tried to protect himself by human devices and all that is left now are decorated tomb walls and a dried-up mummy in a museum!"

If Seti I were the Pharaoh of the Old Testament who treated Jacob's descendents so cruelly, it would have been his daughter who found the baby Moses and brought him to the royal court.

Rameses II followed Seti but was not the eldest son of his father. Was the firstborn son of Seti slain when the angel slew every firstborn in Egypt on the first Passover night? Did Moses grow up together with Rameses II? We don't know for sure, but the Exodus of the children of Israel would fall into the time of that

Pharaoh. If Seti I is the one we think he is, he perhaps used some of his Jewish slaves to build his magnificent tomb.

The traces of Rameses II are found all over Egypt. He is known as an extremely vain king who desired to glorify himself whenever he could. Sometimes he is called "the great chisler," for he had his face inscribed into every statue which existed before him. He erected many statues of himself, one as much as ninety feet tall.

I didn't see his grave but I was told that I would see his most remarkable work and the place for which the world remembers him the most on Wednesday in the great rock temple of Abu Simbel.

The last grave we visited was the tomb of King Tutankhamen, who might not have been significant in his own time, but who is a sensation for our times. Of all the royal tombs in the Valley of the Kings, his is the only one that escaped complete plunder. It was discovered in 1922 by an English archaeologist, Howard Carter. And the description of the discovery is as exciting as the treasures themselves.

Grave robbers had entered the tomb, Carter determined when the tomb was opened, and had left the things in great disorder, but very little had been stolen. He found everything, from the mummy in its many coffins to clothing, jewels, a beautiful throne—everything a Pharoah supposedly needed to live a decent afterlife.

The Americans love King Tut! The traveling exhibition which was, at the time of this writing, in the United States, includes some of Tut's treasures and was sold out in every city where it appeared.

Tut's tomb is the only one we saw where the mummy is still resting in its original place. The mummy cannot be seen. He was left in the huge sarcophagus in a shiny coffin. The golden face on it stares upward with big sad eyes. Those sad dark eyes are hard to forget!

It's hard to die before the age of twenty-one as King Tut did. Even a Pharaoh cannot bargain with death. He came to power at the age of nine or ten and reigned under advisors. The story on the walls of his tomb tell us that he took over and reigned under harsh conditions.

His older brother, Akhenaton, and his brother's beautiful wife, Nefertiti, had upset Egypt's culture by abolishing more than a hundred Egyptian gods, declaring that there was only *one* god, Aton, the sun god, giver of life and abundance. Aton and Akhenaton vanished in less than a generation from history. He has a special spot in my heart for his statue shows that he was a dwarf and badly developed. His artists depicted him in a new, revolutionary way—as a human being, not as a divine god. He and his beautiful wife were obviously dreamers but they left few historic traces.

Tut returned to the old religion and tried to appease the gods "whose hearts were angry in their bodies." He made monuments for all the gods and restored their stories, providing them with gifts and supplying their earthly provisions. He was so busy pleasing the hundred gods of his time that he found no time to prepare his own tomb. About 1340 B.C. Tut died—he had ruled no more then ten years—and workers in the valley had seventy days to get his grave ready. It took that long to prepare the body for its voyage to eternity.

41

During that time eight containers for the mummy were prepared also, one fitting into the next like the layers of an onion or a Chinese Box. The outer shrine measured sixteen feet long and was nine feet high. The coffin itself was solid gold and weighed more than a ton. In the royal cartouch (insignia) of Tutankhamen, and all over the walls of his tomb, one can find the design of ankh, the key of life. It's part of his name, too. He wanted to live so badly, the boy king, and his eyes stare dark, sad and solemn at us from his death mask. A sentence has kept coming back to me and has rung in my heart and mind ever since I heard it first, less than forty-eight hours ago: Here man *thought* that death was vanquished.

January 24—Tuesday Noon

Another early morning flight in a small plane brought us today from Luxor to Aswan. I am still so full from all the things we saw yesterday that I wonder how much more my brain can absorb today. Too many first impressions can become one big jumble which needs to be sorted out at a later time.

Yesterday after the visit at the Valley of the Kings, the guide took us to the funeral temple of Queen Hatshepsut at Deir el-Bahari. It is set in a magnificent natural panorama beneath large cliffs opposite the Valley of the Kings.

The guide obviously didn't like her and had a certain contempt in his voice. After all, a *woman* Pharaoh!

Queen Hatshepsut's temple.

Columns at
Hatshepsut's
temple.
(Notice the
broken noses.)

She didn't inherit the throne from her father Tuthmosis I, he told us. Egyptian hieroglyphs don't even have signs for the name "queen." They have only the sign for "king's great wife." She married her half-brother who died. They had no sons, so the child of her husband and a palace concubine was crowned Tuthmosis III, lord of upper and lower Egypt. She was the power behind the throne for a few years. Then she came forth and declared herself king. In order to convince the people, she claimed that she was not the natural daughter of Tuthmosis I but that her mother had conceived her from the god Amun—the first claim to immaculate conception!

She put the whole love story of her mother and the god, and her birth as a god-child, on the walls of her temple. She also married Tuthmosis III, but was in love with her architect who built the magnificent temple for her. She kept power for two decades, then she died and Tuthmosis III took over. He hated her so much that he defaced and desecrated everything that reminded him of her. The guide showed us how her face or at least her nose is erased in nearly every picture on the walls or on the statues of her. He also showed us a picture of her lover, the architect.

"Betty," I said, while sitting in the airplane and remembering again all the things we had seen and heard the day before, "human nature never changes! Deceit, political intrigue, love affairs—nothing changes under the sun, does it?"

Betty smiled and nodded.

"Poor thing," I grinned, "she was a bit ahead of her time. Today she would have an easier time pulling the whole thing off. The women's liberation movement

44

would probably make her their honorary president. She wouldn't have to wear a false beard or man's clothing either."

"The beard was a sign of wisdom and was artificially worn by any Pharaoh," Betty said. "It's also interesting to see that not only *her* nose was erased but most statues or pictures of *any* Pharaoh have missing noses. A guide told me on my last visit that the Egyptians have always believed that the spirit of a person comes and goes through the nose. So if one did not want to be bothered by the spirit of his ancestor any longer, the nose of his statue or picture was smashed. Remember, even the sphinx has a smashed-up nose."

Yes, I tried hard to remember the many things I had seen and also to prepare myself for the things ahead.

On the way to the hotel we visited the Aswan quarries and Betty and I climbed all over the unfinished obelisk. One hundred thirty-seven feet long and fourteen feet thick at the base, it's the same rose-color granite we had seen in other places in stones and statues. But this obelisk had been abandoned by the ancient stonecutters because it had cracked in the wrong place after it was nearly finished.

"How did they cut such hard rock so effectively?" I asked Betty. The sides were as smooth as glass.

"They began by chiseling notches into the rock, then they wedged wood into the depressions and either burned the wood to heat the rock and then poured water over the rock to crack it, or they wet the wood to swell it to the point where it split the rock.

"Whatever or however the ancients did it, they did it so perfectly that they could build without mortar or cement. The pyramids and many other monuments we saw are put together by perfectly sitting stones that are so tight not even the blade of a knife can penetrate the cracks!" Betty explained. Every so often I feel overwhelmed by what I see and hear.

Now we were getting ready to see a modern monument of ingenious building in Egypt, and the Pharaohs would have been proud of it. It's on the grandeur of a Rameses scale: the Aswan High Dam.

Betty and I had been looking forward to seeing the dam more than any other place in Egypt. There seemed to be great differences in opinion about the benefits and the problems it created for Egypt. We were most eager to see for ourselves.

The high dam was built in the sixties when superdams were the popular thing all over the world. Lake Nasser, created by the high dam, drowned Nubia. But scientists promised the reclaiming of a million acres from Egypt's desert and an increase of from one to three crops each year on an additional seven hundred thousand acres. Twelve electric turbines would spin out ten billon kilowatt hours of electricity annually to power new industries for Egypt. Above all, the dam would conserve water from wet years to help irrigate through dry years.

It sounded fantastic and everybody was for it. The Russians financed the project and provided more than eight hundred engineers and technicians to guide the work. A work force of thirty thousand men, people of many nations, worked together to make this miracle of modern technology come true.

It was finished in July of 1970. The monarch who asked for the dam did not witness its completion. Nasser died and Sadat, together with a Russian, inaugurated the dam on Nasser's fifty-third birthday.

Nasser had promised that Egypt would pay the loan and the interest back to Russia within three years of the completion of the dam. This was to be possible because of the increased national income from agricultural and industrial developments.

Betty had followed the news about the dam for the last decade. Leading American magazines like *Newsweek*, *Reader's Digest*, *Time*, *Life* and others had occasionally given a report on that super dam and, according to the United States news media, the Aswan dam has caused nothing but grave problems ever since its completion. We tried to ask our host and the guide about some of the things Betty had read previously, but nobody gave us any clear-cut answers.

"How do *you* feel about the high dam?" I had asked Mr. Hermina when we got ready to fly to Aswan. "Is it good or bad for Egypt?"

"It's neither," he shrugged, "it's a nuisance, that's all! We wouldn't have the thing if John Foster Dulles hadn't pulled out on us. We had no choice but to accept the Russian's help. It was Nasser's big idea to make himself famous."

"But it's hurting your farmers in lower Egypt, isn't it?" I dug again.

"Why should it?" our host asked surprised.

We figured that the man either had no idea or he acted ignorant. So we decided to find out for ourselves.

Well, the driver who will take us, finally, to the high dam is honking his car horn. We had to get special permission and cut some red tape to enter military-restricted areas. We have been cleared and here we go!

47

January 24—
Late Tuesday Evening

We returned from our visit to the dam and I have another nervous lump in my throat and knots in my stomach. Betty and I went to see with open minds and eagerness to find the true facts. We came back never to be the same again. I shall *never* forget that visit!

Wondering if the American press exaggerated the problems *because* the United States and Britain had withdrawn from the project in 1956, giving the Russians the opportunity to be the "good neighbor," we were ready to ask and to listen in an unbiased way.

The Egyptian chief engineer, who spoke fluent English, personally took us around. Proudly he gave us the well-known facts about size and proportions.

"Sadd el Ali" as the Egyptians call it, is one of the world's largest dams and has the biggest hydro-electric power station in the world. It is an earthen dam, one mile wide at the base, thirty-six stories high and more than two-and-a-half miles long. Fifty-two million cubic yards of rock, sand and mud were used as filling, equal in bulk to seventeen Cheops pyramids. A broad highway runs across the top. We drove it, stopped, took pictures and finally settled in the engineer's office for additional questioning.

The lake behind the dam interested us the most. We knew the Egyptians had a problem filling it with water to its capacity.

I took the bull by the horns with my first question: "Do you consider the dam beneficial for Egypt?" I asked with a smile.

The dam built by the Russians at Lake Nasser.

Lake Nasser showing island where Russian scientists live.

"Of course," the young man said. "It will help Egypt to a better future, as soon as we can reclaim and irrigate large desert areas."

"Do you think the lake will ever fill to capacity?" I asked next.

"We are confident to have it filled by 1982," he said with great ease.

I decided not to put him on the defensive by pointing out that it was supposed to have been filled by 1970. Some scientists like Professor Abdel Goker think that it may take another two hundred years; others believe it will never fill.

"How high is your evaporation factor?" Betty asked.

"Ten percent, madam," he said, giving her a surprised look. He obviously didn't expect such detailed questions.

"Is the evaporation bigger than was expected and does it create a problem?" Betty asked next.

"Not really, the scientists had anticipated it and it is of no great consequence."

Betty and I kept silent. We didn't try to embarrass him by letting him know that we were aware of the fact that the evaporation was fifty percent more than the Russian engineers had anticipated. They had forgotten to calculate the high wind velocity on such a large body of water. The lake is 310 miles long and the surface equals two thousand square miles. I remembered something Betty had mentioned to me about that. The lake was squandering incredible amounts of water—not only by evaporation into the dry hot desert air but also by seepage into the west shore, which is porous limestone. (Fifteen billion cubic meters a year evaporate, which is one half of what used to go into the sea. Thirty billion cubic meters a year run away into underground rivers in the desert, useless to civilization anywhere. The loss by seepage alone is one-third of all the water that flows into the lake.)

I tried to change the subject. "Is it a fact that all the silt that enriched Egypt every year, when the Nile flooded, sinks now to the bottom of the lake, benefiting nobody?"

"Yes, madam," he said, "it is true but we can easily redeem that with fertilizers. It is a cheap price to pay for the advantages of Egypt's future."

I looked at that young man and wondered. Did he really not know the devastating facts or was he just not willing to lose face for his country in front of two American women?

Before the building of the dam the Nile flooded one hundred million tons of silt every year over the cultivated areas of Egypt. Now the six million acres of farmland need fertilizer at a cost of one hundred million dollars a year. The problem is that the farmers of lower Egypt don't have the money for it and the land goes sour. There are less crops and more mouths to feed among the people. The average peasant in Cairo lives on sixteen cents a day.

I knew that was true because I had seen the poverty of the farmers everywhere. We watched them scrape the fertile earth off the edges of the canals outside of Cairo. Donkeys carried the soil, which contained the last bit of silt, in small saddle pouches to the farmers' little patches of land. When there is nothing left to scrape, what will happen to them?

The Nile is now clear, so clear that one Egyptian agriculturist said: "I'd give my soul to turn it [the Nile] muddy brown again." Clear Nile water makes magnificent night scenes but very poor soil.

I had another question: "We saw that the canals in lower Egypt are empty, don't you have enough irrigation water?"

"Of course, madam," the man said, "we have more than enough water, but right now little is needed. It's harvest time!" He got up to leave. We got up, too.

"Where are the spillways for the dam?" Betty asked nonchalantly.

"Over there," said the engineer and pointed toward the turbines.

"May I take a picture?" Betty asked.

"Of course," he said politely, but a bit uneasily.

He turned to me. "It is true that lower Egypt has some inconveniences at the present time because of the dam but it will help upper Egypt into a better future. President Sadat hopes to settle more than a million-and-a-half people in our area and the water will be pumped out to irrigate the land to grow crops."

I didn't argue with the friendly man. I realized that I would get no objective answers anyway. I decided not to ask any more embarrassing questions either. I didn't ask if it was true that the Russians had not provided extra spillways and the twelve turbines were the *only* outlet the dam had. I didn't point out that lower Egypt needed ten billion cubic meters of water more than they were getting right now to irrigate their land. I didn't ask why only *two* turbines were working as we stood and observed. I didn't say that it made little sense to me to help upper Egypt when most of the Egyptians lived in the lower Nile valley and the delta.

I also did not let him know that we were aware of the

threat the delta faced. The salinity of the Mediterranean Sea is rising because it receives only a very small portion of the previous sweet waters of the Nile. That kills the fish. (Egypt now loses eighteen thousand tons of sardines a year because one-fifth of the catch has disappeared!) Not only is Egypt affected but the whole eastern shore of the Mediterranean Sea. For six hundred miles fishermen have fishing problems.

The salt water is slowly seeping into the marshlands of the delta, decreasing productivity of the land by as much as fifty percent. Unless the underground waters can be drained, millions of acres will turn to brown rubble within the next decade.

On top of all this there is an increased rodent population in the dry canals and an explosion of water-borne diseases in lower Egypt. Egypt always had snails that carry a parasite called *bilharzia,* (a prickly blood fluke). As long as the Nile flooded the land and canals every year, the snails were washed out to the sea and kept under control. Now snails and parasites multiply rapidly, so rapidly that bilharziasis has grown to epidemic proportions. Nobody knows how many have it. One American magazine claims that fourteen million of the thirty-seven million Egyptians are affected; another writes that one of every two people carries the parasite in the blood.

When the parasite gets into human blood it multiplies rapidly and forever. There is no lasting cure known so far and the affected person lives with great pain and increasing exhaustion. It's so contagious that a healthy person setting foot into infected water may pick up flukes without a bite or scratch. Infected persons are too weak to work more than a few hours a

53

day. One out of every ten Egyptians supposedly dies right now of bilharziasis, a sickness known to the Pharaohs of ancient times.

And then, there are. . . .

Problems, problems, problems, and more problems!

I decided to ask one more question. "Why did Egypt kick all the Russians out? When my friend," pointing to Betty, "visited this place the last time in 1969, the place swarmed with Russian soldiers and every sign was written in Russian and Arabic. Now we see no Russians and all your signs read in Arabic and English. What caused the break?"

The engineer threw up his hands in utter horror: "Madam," he said, "I cannot answer. This is a political question. However, we do have four or five Russian scientists still living here. They oversee the dam."

"If you need to ask them something, how do you communicate? Do you speak Russian?" I asked.

"No, madam," he said. "We call our government in Cairo. They call the Russian embassy in Cairo. The embassy calls Moscow. Moscow calls the Russian engineers here in Aswan. Then the process is reversed and we finally receive an answer through Cairo. However, we do greet each other and exchange some simple phrases when our paths cross."

We all smiled and I knew it was time to leave. We shook hands and the car drove slowly once more across the top of the dam so Betty could take some more pictures of the enormous lake. It wasn't full but it carried an awful lot of water. It stands 364 feet above the bed of the Nile and 643 feet above sea level.

Suddenly a ghastly thought struck me, "What if—?"

"Remind me to ask you something when we get to

the hotel room," I murmured under my breath to Betty.

As soon as we were alone, I asked Betty the question that bothered me. "Betty, has anyone ever thought of what would happen if that dam ever breaks, either by natural disaster or by attack of war through bombing or sabotage?"

"I don't know if the Egyptians have ever thought about it. I know that a German writer has. He wrote a novel called *Aswan* (by Michael Heim. New York: Alfred A. Knopf, Inc., 1972). It's now translated into English and I want you to read it when we get home. It's a chilling book. I am sure the Egyptians have banned it. It could cause unrest and hysteria in the land. The author suggests that in case of a dam break a ten-foot wall of water would bury Cairo and the Mediterranean Sea would have a rise in sea level as far as Italy."

"Don't say any more, Betty," I said. "This whole story of the dam makes me sick. I realize that the American magazines told us things the average Egyptians don't know. But their leaders know! Betty, Egypt is in trouble, economically, defense-wise and politically. And I would like to know *why* Sadat kicked the Russians out, but nobody will tell us."

January 25— Wednesday Afternoon

This morning we flew from Aswan to Abu Simbel and returned from there to Cairo by early evening.

55

Another over-full day that raised more questions in my mind for which I don't seem to find all the answers.

The morning flight took us along Lake Nasser for more than twenty-five minutes. When we landed in Abu Simbel we were near the Sudan border and still had not seen the end of the lake. Like an ocean the dammed-up waters of the Nile spread in all four directions. The lake itself reaches deep into Sudanian deserts, I was told. And Nasser's Egypt had promised to pay Sudan for giving up huge desert lands to create the lake. They haven't been able to pay their debts either to Russia or Sudan. The lake has not yet brought in the additional income Egypt had anticipated.

Lake Nasser reminds me of an ocean not only because the waters are so very deep, emerald blue and clear, but also because the shores look like beaches. Where the waters end, the sand begins. The shores show no sign of green growth or life. No villages have been built near the water, no fields are cultivated around the lake. The air view shows endless stretches of water and lifeless golden-brown dunes of deep sand, as far as the eye can see.

Something about the scene gave me a feeling of great concern again. I bent toward Betty who sat beside the window taking pictures. "Betty," I asked, "how come there is no sign of life along the shores of this lake? When we flew along the Nile in lower Egypt, a green strip marked the Nile valley from the air. Why is there nothing growing around the lake, not even weeds, cacti or desert bushes?"

"First of all, remember the evaporation rate I asked for when we talked with the chief engineer?" Betty said and she looked as troubled as I felt. "The waterline is obviously changing from day to day, so nobody can anticipate where the water will end at any given time. The lake hasn't filled as predicted and the desert winds evaporate at a greater rate than the engineers expected. So the lake has no constant water level, ever. That means that the Nubian tribes who were relocated just temporarily outside their former land, which is now at the bottom of the lake, cannot be brought back to the shores. The water level changes too fast and could either flood their villages or, more often, leave them high and dry.

"The other problem which I never realized until I saw it with my own eyes," Betty continued, "is that sand and water don't grow *anything*. The sand has to be mixed with soil to produce crops. The Nile valley of lower Egypt has received soil from the silt of the overflowing Nile for thousands of years. Therefore it is green. As far as the silt has been spread by the river, the land produces. The Nile is now depositing all its silt at the bottom of the lake, and it does nobody any good at all anymore.

"If Sadat is planning to bring one-and-a-half million Egyptians up here to live, he will not only have to solve the problems of an ever-changing shoreline, but he will have to bring in soil from somewhere. The Sahara Desert grows food only when sand, soil and water are present. Up here one ingredient is missing. That is obvious."

It was more obvious to us after we had landed and a bus took us to the shores of Lake Nasser and we walked up to the temples of Abu Simbel.

Our guide was a delight to be with. He spoke fluent

57

English, had a degree in archaeology from the University of Cairo and acted most eager to show us anything and everything. It was not part of his usual lecture, but a passing remark hooked deep into the growing uneasiness of my troubled soul and bothered me. He pointed to a pitiful-looking patch of young grass that withered in the desert sun and sharp winds and said smilingly: "Someday when we learn how to grow grass up here, this whole area shall be transformed and look green and beautiful. We have great plans for this area."

I had a hard time following his lecture after that. I couldn't shake a strange feeling that day I was seeing not only some famous ancient temples but the fulfillment of Old Testament prophecies in a present-day setting.

Betty and I had read some Bible texts in our morning devotion. She showed them to me after I expressed my perturbed thoughts to her.

"Why would *one* man like Nasser dare to alter the life of Egypt as deeply as he has," I said, still distressed after what we had observed at the dam the day before. "Weren't there *any* scientists who warned the Egyptians? Didn't anyone foresee some of the problems such a dam would bring?"

"Yes," Betty said, "there was supposedly *one* Egyptian scientist who predicted disaster, but Nasser kicked him out of the country. I read somewhere that America pulled out of the dam project because the statement of that scientist raised some questions with the United States government of that time."

"Am I ever glad they did listen," I said. "I am sure that we Americans would feel not only responsible but guilty if we had built such a monstrosity. But why would *one* man be permitted to make such far-reaching decisions for a whole land as Nasser was? This mistake cannot be changed ever! The Nile will *never* distribute silt again. The Mediterranean Sea will *never* receive enough river water to reverse the damages. The delta will sour more and more, and Egypt will suffer for all generations to come because *one* man thought he owned the Nile. The whole thing is irreversible!" It was then that Betty handed me her open Bible, pointed to a text and said, "Remember that Nasser was a dictator and the Egyptians since ancient times are used to being ruled by autocrats. You have lived in a democracy too long by now to remember what it is like to have *one* person run a whole country. No doubt about it, Nasser thought he owned Egypt and the Nile. But God can never agree with that. This is what I started to read aloud from the nineteenth chapter of Isaiah:

And the waters from the sea will dry up, and the river will be parched and dry. And the canals will emit a stench, the streams of Egypt will thin out and dry up; the reeds and rushes will rot away. The bulrushes by the Nile, by the edge of the Nile and all the sown fields by the Nile will become dry, be driven away, and be no more. And the fishermen will lament, and all those who cast a line into the Nile will mourn, and those who spread nets on the waters will pine away. (verses 5–8)."

Next she found Ezekiel 29 and pointed to the following texts:

59

The word of the Lord came to me saying, "Son of man, set your face against Pharaoh king of Egypt, and prophesy against him and against all Egypt. Speak and say, 'Thus says the Lord God, "Behold, I am against you, Pharaoh king of Egypt, the great monster that lies in the midst of his rivers, that has said, 'My Nile is mine, and I myself have made it.' And I shall put hooks in your jaws, and I shall make the fish of your rivers cling to your scales. And I shall bring you up out of the midst of your rivers, and all the fish of your rivers will cling to your scales. And I shall abandon you to the wilderness, you and all the fish of your rivers; you will fall on the open field; you will not be brought together or gathered. I have given you for food to the beasts of the earth and to the birds of the sky. Then all the inhabitants of Egypt will know that I am the Lord, because they have been only a staff made of reeds to the house of Israel. When they took hold of you with the hand, you broke and tore all their hands; and when they leaned on you, you broke and made all their loins quake."

Therefore thus says the Lord God, "Behold I shall bring upon you a sword and I shall cut off from you man and beast. And the land of Egypt will become a desolation and waste. Then they will know that I am the Lord. Because you said, 'The Nile is mine, and I have made it,' therefore, behold, I am against you and against your rivers, and I will make the land of Egypt an utter waste and desolation, from Migdol to Syene and even to the border of Ethiopia' " (verses 1-10).

I handed her the Bible and didn't know what to say I felt so overcome.

Oh, the timelessness of God's Word and its principles which can be applied at *any* time! Nasser would have done well to realize that God's prophetic truth meant him as well as the ancient Pharaohs. Oh, what hardship millions of simple people have suffered and will yet suffer, because one lone dictator ignored God's advice! I couldn't help but wonder if that has been the story of Egypt all along.

To enter the temples of Abu Simbel is to wonder how many thousands of slaves Rameses II brought into the deadly heat of the upper Egypt desert to glorify one man's vain name.

I felt great relief to find for a change two temples, not more tombs, that told the story of the great chisler and builder Rameses II, the Pharaoh of the exodus of the Old Testament. The size of Abu Simbel is overpowering. The sanctuary itself was cut 180 feet deep into the living rock and the interior is dominated by eight huge statues of Rameses II. Smaller chambers surround the immense main sanctuary. The heights are staggering. And every inch of it has been carved out of the rocks! Most of the wall carvings are colored and depict the life and death story of one man. They show the wars and battles of the king, his conquests and his triumphs, his victories and his great fame. But that is not all.

Rameses II decided to be more than all the other Pharaohs. He not only declared himself the king, but the temple walls tell the story of a Pharaoh who decided to become also the high priest of his land and finally a god among the Egyptian gods.

The innermost sanctuary (called the holy of holies by our Egyptian guide) shows four gods sitting in equal dignity on one massive throne, carved out of the living rock. In front of them is a cube of a rock where the priests and the king-high priest, Rameses II, came to worship. And who were the four gods that Pharaoh worshiped?

Ra Harakhte, the god of the rising sun who restored eternal after-life and whose crown is a sun disk; Aman-Re, the chief of the gods and the one who created everything—he wears the highest crown of all; Ptah, the god of wisdom, who wears no outer crown because his mind *is* his crown. Then betweeen Ra Harakhte and Aman-Re sits Rameses II—with the crown of upper and lower Egypt—as a god equal to Egypt's leading gods.

I looked stunned at the four figures. Did I hear the guide tell the story right? A man, a human being built a temple in which his living self came to worship his deified self? I interrupted the guide: "Are you saying that Rameses II came into this temple to worship himself during his own lifetime?"

"Yes, madam," the eager guide explained, "and not only that, he had the temple built at such an angle that on two days of each year, February 23 and October 23, the rays of the rising sun reach down into the inner-most sanctuary and light up the face of the god Rameses II and part of the holy of holies!"

Rameses also decided to share his new deity with his favorite wife, Nefertari. She was a daughter of his who he married before he became the Pharaoh. He built her a smaller temple right next to his own to tell the story of immortal deity for his queen. The carvings on

Temple at Abu Simbel.

Find Hansi
at the
foot of
the statue
of Rameses
at Abu
Simbel.

the wall tell how he made himself the intercessor between the gods and his wife and how they accepted his request and received her into the imperishable line of gods.

Betty nudged me while we listened and looked. She had never been in Abu Simbel previously either and the whole thing overpowered both of us. "Do you realize what we are seeing right now?" she said softly. "God's incarnation and plan of salvation in reverse. God became *man* to save the human race. Whenever the great enemy of God has a chance to rule, he will mock God and reverse God's plan or design. Here man made himself a god and he also made the mind, the intellect, to reign supreme."

I nodded, "Well, from the sign of the cross as the ankh to the immaculate conception of Hatshepsut to Rameses II being an intercessor for others while worshiping intellect and self, Satan has managed to create quite a counterfeit to the genuine design of God, hasn't he? And he never changes his approaches, only the methods vary. Modern men worship the intellect and self at the altar of science as devoutly as Rameses did when he brought honey, food and flowers to himself and his fellow gods."

I shall never forget Abu Simbel. I am glad they saved those famous sites. The waters of the dammed-up Nile threatened to destroy it as the lake began to fill. Egypt turned to the United Nations for help to preserve these irreplaceable ancient structures and people from all over the world came to save it.

America financed much of the bold plan which moved the temples from the original sites to higher ground. It took many millions of dollars and great manpower to accomplish the task. The statues, pillars and sides were cut into blocks and moved by huge cranes to the top of the cliff where they were assembled in their former design.

Modern architecture almost lost the buildings anyway because the ancient stone cutters had built the temples so perfectly that the reassembling of the stones could not be copied in our times. A huge cement dome had to be built above the reconstructed temples to hold it all together. An artificial mound hides the cement dome and the temples rise as they have risen before only on higher ground. Even the angles are the same so that the first sun rays of the two days in February and October still touch the stone face of the god Rameses II.

It's exciting—and a bit depressing. The ancient Egyptians said, "To speak of the dead is to make them live again."

Yes, they did accomplish what they set out to do. After thousands of years the world still speaks of these vanished civilizations. The names of Rameses II and Seti are still alive for archaeologists and some curious world travelers of today. How meager an afterlife it is, however, in comparison to the effort that was made to secure immortality!

How many slaves had to die in the cruel desert heat for it? How many lips cursed the name of the Pharaoh under their breath while giving every ounce of life and strength to immortalize him?

Yes, here men *thought* that death was vanquished!

January 26—Thursday Evening

I am so glad that the taping of the international TV program has been changed from 10:00 P.M. tonight to 10:00 A.M. tomorrow morning. I wondered how I would hold up so late and still be alert enough to appear alive on the screen. I am dead tired!

This was a strange day. It's obvious by now that we shall not be able to meet President Sadat; he is getting ready to fly to the United States to meet President Carter. In his place we had this morning an interview with the head of the Centre for Political and Strategic Studies. He appears to be one of the most influential representatives of the intellectual class in Egypt and one of the strong voices of the entire Arab world.

He permitted me most graciously to tape our conversation on our little cassette recorder. I told him that I didn't want to misquote him when I wrote my book on the Middle East. So he knew that I was recording, but at the end of our long interview I wondered whether he still remembered that his words were all on tape. Maybe he did. It is hard to figure out the mind of a man of the Middle East. Did he contradict President Sadat deliberately or did his aggressive remarks about America and Israel come out at an unguarded moment?

Here are some of the questions I asked and his answers as we have them on our tapes:

Hansi: Then, you feel that the colonial powers tried to develop only the servant role of your people?

Arab Leader: Yes. And this is the story of colonialism all over the world, the third world.

H.: True. I agree with you.

A.L.: If we are not to have a comparative approach.—Sometimes some European countries, when they invaded some countries in the third world, these invaded countries were more developed culturally than the invading countries.

H.: I agree with you on that. There is no doubt about it, you have the most glorious history.

A.L.: Right, right. And this is an obstacle now. This memory of this glorious history is one of our obstacles. Yes. Afterwards in the fifties we tried to gain our independence. In the age of Nasser, Nasser tried to build and strengthen the abilities of the Egyptians and the Arabs in general to have their own role in international politics. While one may criticize Nasser for so many things, internally or externally, one cannot understand this phenomenon—this charismatic leader—Abdul Nasser, without stressing the fact that he was the symbol of the dignity of the Arabs. He was the symbol of the dignity of the Arabs, and he entered into the international scene through a national project trying to defend the interest of the Arabs, trying to show that one, even in a small country like Egypt or a small area like the Arab world, we should guard our independence, we should play our role, a positive role in achieving peace in the world. But here again we find another obstacle. Israel played a negative role, it was an obstacle for the development of Egypt and for some other Arab countries.

H.: The question now is, in what way can other super powers, like America, and the people thereof be helpful in developing your goals.

A.L.: Well, I think this is an important question. I

would like to have an American/Arab dialogue similiar to the European/Arab dialogue.

H.: I see. Who is mainly in the European/Arab dialogue? The British or Germans?

A.L.: No. The whole European community, represented by the community. There is an Arab team represented by the Arab league. You may be astonished if I told you that some Egyptians are not able to grasp some of the most important Egyptian problems. Perhaps we Egyptian intellectuals have an accurate idea about the structure and function of the American society. We have an accurate idea but I doubt if so many Americans have the same idea in general of the Arab society in general, or the Egyptian society.

H.: Why would you feel that you have the accurate idea about the Americans? Have you studied into it?

A.L.: No. But one important remark that you should know, the bulk of sociological research is affected by the American school. Don't forget a very important thing for the masses is the American movie. The American movie was responsible to give the Egyptians a fair idea about the American style of life.

H.: Now, if I may take exception to that. I personally feel that the American movies do not represent America. I feel that American movies are doing tremendous harm to the American representation in the world. Because having known the European background and the American background, having lived in America for more than twenty years, I get furious at what they represent. I'm very sad about that. Your specialists should not go by that only for it would be only one aspect of the area.

A.L.: Of course, I said the masses. One thing about that is the American movie played a negative aspect in our masses.

H.: Amen. Have they ever!

A.L.: One of their ideas of this American style of life, you see, is a negative aspect of these American movies. In a poor country like Egypt they feel that this is splendid, this is the way of life, which is not represented really, as you have said.

H.: Yes, but you see, sir, your dialogue on the intellectual level, on the educated level, very often does not reach the masses. At least, not in America.

A.L.: But if we begin these dialogues, discussing the cultural aspects, the political aspects, the economic aspects, this will give the frame of reference.

H.: OK. I can buy that.

A.L.: But the most important thing which is very difficult, and I know it, is how public opinion in your country is formulated.

H.: It is formulated by the news.

A.L.: Yes, I know. But who are controlling the news? Who are giving the Americans the news? This is a very complicated problem. And through this media, this biased, this distorted image of Egyptians and Arabs are through these systems of control, controlling the minds of the Americans.

H.: You don't mind if I quote you on that?

A.L.: Yes. You may quote me. Of course.

H.: I agree with you on that. It is one of my pet peeves. One of my greatest concerns is that somebody right now is controlling the media in America in a way that we do not quite get two sides of the story any more.

69

A.L.: There is a specific point of the Zionist control in France. I speak of France because I have studied in France and in Milan. The Zionists control of the mass media, so many Zionists, French Zionists, working at the newspapers, television, and especially on the radio.

H.: Your experience is in France. And you have not had too much experience with Britain then?

A.L.: No. For the States, there is another example. You find this control, the Zionist control in the States is very clear. You find the Zionist lobby at the Congress. Every time when Egypt—Egypt is trying now to buy weapons from the States, will be faced immediately by the Zionist's lobby at the congress, immediately.

H.: Now, do you feel that President Carter will be able to break through that?

A.L.: Well, he is trying. And I think one of the reasons of the initiatives of Sadat to go to Israel was that he perceived that Carter was stuck at the moment by this lobby. The Zionist lobby in the States was able to stop Carter because he was willing to accelerate the processes of peace. This was against the interests of Israel. He wanted to jump this obstacle by going directly to Israel to have their concessions. The Israelis are going to stop the processes of peace by presenting some procedural problems about committees to consume the time.

H.: What will happen if these peace talks do not succeed?

A.L.: Which peace talks?

H.: Between the two Middle East powers.

A.L.: Obviously, what do you think?

H.: Well, I know that the superpowers will be pulled

into it. If that happens it could mean World War III. And I think this is the great concern of the American people right now. Nobody wants war. You don't want it. You don't need it. I see your country, you don't need war. You need peace. You need development and progress.

A.L.: The Israelis are not interested in peace. They need the land.

H.: This is a tremendous concern for everybody. And I am not the politician to decide. Everybody hopes that Carter will have enough of an influence to settle this thing. And make everybody give in so that they can meet in the middle.

A.L.: How can we meet in the middle? We are very modest in our demands. We want our land. Just like that. We want our land which is defended internationally. And we are interested to give the most specific guarantees to Israel—to guarantee the security. But here again, the Israelis said, "There are settlements in Sinai, we would like to keep the settlements in your land and be defended by the Israeli forces." This will be refused without compromise. This is related to the Egyptian history against colonialism. We are very sensitive to two things: colonialism and withdrawal. When we were children at our schools we used to go shouting in the streets to begin the withdrawal of the British from our country. These two terms, occupation and withdrawal, are basic in our modern history. It is a very sensitive thing for the Egyptians. Never will we leave one centimeter from our land. And if the Israelis do not withdraw another war will be launched—even after twenty years. Because we are not so powerful now, compared to the very sophisticated planes which

71

the United States sold to Israel. One week ago 115 planes, the most sophisticated planes, were given by the States to Israel at this very crucial moment. How can you explain that? Even after Israel has shown that she is not interested in peace, you give to the Israelis. You the States. And you are making them more stubborn than ever. How can you explain that? Is the States interested in keeping peace in the area? Or, which is called the even-handed policy in the area? How can you explain this huge military thing, even to the Israelis?

H.: So you feel that Israel is the new colonial power that is trying to come into your land, take your land away?

A.L.: No. This is not a new colonial power. We have our old explanation for the Israelis. It is a typical example of what you call the colonial-settler regime.

H.: Which you are very sensitive to?

A.L.: Not very sensitive, but because they are trying to take our land.

H.: You know, there has not always been that kind of strife or conflict between the Israeli and the Egyptian. In olden times you had Jewish settlements hiding here in Egypt.

A.L.: This is another problem. We have no problem with the Jews as Jews.

H.: You don't?

A.L.: No. But we have problems with the Zionists and Israelis who are trying to take our land.

H.: So you have Jews—

A.L.: We have no case with the Jews. The problem is against Zionists which means expansion, racial discrimination against the Arabs. This is our problem.

Now, through this initiative of Sadat, what do we want? We want to arrive to external compromise. Although we know that Zionism is a national ideology, that this type of society wants expansion, we would like to arrive at this compromise: we will give you the recognition that you are a part of this area; give us our land and take our guarantees for your security. This is a very simple plan presented by Sadat. It was refused.

H.: Well, when it comes to politics, there isn't too much I feel that I understand. And I think that the American people are right now very confused. Whatever I write, I always introduce the human interest that we are people, that we are all brothers on this continent. We are not an island. We all are brothers on this globe. We are all together and we must learn to work together. I've dedicated my life to bring that international understanding and that international friendship to the people.

I felt physically ill when we left the plush conference room where the interview had been given. Betty looked into my face, "Are you okay?"

I nodded. I had asked for tea without sugar but the servant had served sticky sweet tea to all of us. I had to drink it. One does not dare to refuse a drink or any offered food without offending the host gravely. Eating and drinking together is a sign of friendship in the Middle East culture. So we all drank sugary sweet tea together, even though sugar makes me sick. But I wasn't so sure it was the sugar alone which made me feel so miserable.

As soon as I could speak to Betty under my breath, I said, "Betty, I know now what bothers me so deeply here in Cairo. What I see and hear in this city reminds me of Nazi Germany. The banners carry similar phrases to those the Germans had for Adolph Hitler. What the man said about going to get 'their' land—even if they had to wait until they had more military power—Hitler used the same words. I still can hear him shout that Germany needed *lebensraum* (room to live) and would go for former German territory as soon as the land was strong enough. The Germans believed Hitler and that began World War II! They never got their *lebensraum* but lost much of what they had before, and the world ended up in a blood bath in the process.

"I cannot help but wonder if these are the first signs that World War III is brewing in the minds of some Middle East leaders. This man has no doubt more influence upon the Arab world than Sadat has. According to his answers, this Arab leader was here under Nasser. He most likely will be here after Sadat has gone. Who knows who will be in the president's seat of Egypt tomorrow? But the leaders of Egypt's educated class remain and decide what the masses will be taught, regardless of who is in the president's seat. This man is no friend of Israel or America. He is pro-Nasser, which means he is pro-Russian! I surely would like to know why Sadat is in such great enmity with the Russians. What are the true motivations behind all the peace talks Egypt presents right now to the world? Something does not ring true—or am I too sensitive due to my own misguided past?"

Betty couldn't answer because we walked into the waiting hall of another government official of the highest influence.

"He is the minister of foreign affairs," Mr. Hermina told us. "We have two in that position, one carries the title, the other does most of the work. You are meeting the one who carries the greater weight."

We sat and waited for several hours. I assured everybody that my business was not urgent enough to take any more valuable time away from such a busy man. But it seemed most important to Mr. Hermina and the government guide that we have an audience with this man.

When we were finally ushered in, I apologized to the foreign minister for taking his time and told him that I would only stay for a few short minutes.

I did! I also asked for permission to tape our interview. He smiled politely and denied my request. "We can talk easier without it." he said. So we did!

We chatted for a little while with small talk. Then I asked him if the Arab world was really as mad at Egypt and President Sadat as the United States press said in our newspapers.

He shook his head and smiled again. "No," he said, "we understand each other and we try to help one another."

"Do you see Egypt as the leader of the Arab countries?" I asked.

"No," he said evasively, "we don't see ourselves as the leaders. We just try to encourage the Arab world to work together. We also begin now to make friends with some nations in Africa. I just met with an African ambassador for several hours. That's the reason you had to wait so long.

"I believe strongly," he continued "that the Third World will and must unite so that we may help each other. Then we don't need to depend upon the super-powers any more."

I thanked him kindly and got up to leave. I knew that we were of no use to each other. So why should I waste his precious time. I was sorry I didn't have our interview on tape, but what could I do? I was the guest in a foreign land and had to submit to his will. I felt so sad that people cannot trust each other just because they represent a different nation and nationality. Though a private citizen I represented the United States to him, while he stood for the opinions of Egypt as a leader—and as a human being.

I looked at him and realized that we could have never seen eye to eye even if we had tried. His culture and mine are too different. His way of thinking and mine are oceans apart. I can put myself into his frame of reference because I once lived in similar circumstances as Egypt has right now, but an Egyptian can *never* follow the thinking of an American, unless he has lived in America for some time. The American life-style is so unique that nobody in the rest of the big wide world lives and thinks like the American people. That in itself brings great misunderstanding. It took me years to follow and adopt the American way of thinking while living in the New World.

The key to the difference in points of view is America's freedom. People who are permitted to think for themselves and decide the destiny of their land by their inner restraint, those who permit themselves to be governed by God instead of being ruled by dictators and tyrants, react and act differently than a people who are used to bondage and oppression.

The leaders of both lands think differently and so

do the common people. American government leaders have in the past made grave errors because they couldn't follow the way their friends and foes around the world think.

I could not help but be greatly concerned about the upcoming meetings between our American president and Sadat. I prayed that God would give them both wisdom and discernment to look past the other person's culture to the true intentions of each other's heart.

I wish the whole atmosphere around here wouldn't remind me so much of the time when Germany shouted, "Peace, peace," just before World War II lashed out. I pray that Sadat wants real peace, not revenge as Hitler did!

January 28—Saturday
Afternoon, En Route to Jordan

What a day to finish our visit to Egypt!

Yesterday ended up being almost a lost day. We spent most of it in a drafty TV studio. We waited from 10:00 A.M. to 2:00 P.M. for the TV crew and the interviewer to appear. Friday is the Moslem's holy day and nobody shows up for work until the noon prayer hour is over. Why we were asked to show up in the morning is one of the many puzzles I shall never know.

The interviewer was a flashy young man dressed in Western corduroys and bright knit shirt and extremely high-heeled shoes. He spoke fluent English and acted rather self-assured. I was told that he was one of Egypt's most popular and highest-paid actors. Everybody seemed to be in deepest awe before him—except we two little old ladies from America! That amused him greatly. We took a liking to each other—the actor and I—and we ended up with a spirited and lively international program which pleased both of us.

The late taping did not permit us to do what I wanted to do in the afternoon: visit the Suez Canal. I was disappointed but I have learned to be flexible and trust God's plans for my days.

We spent this morning in the Cairo museum—without escort. It took some manuevering on our part but I was rather determined to do it *our* way for a change. I knew what we wanted to see and what to look for and I didn't want our guide or host to choose for us, as they had all along.

So we declined graciously to be driven or taken and we walked from the hotel to the museum on our own.

First we went to the mummy room. I had never seen a mummy before and wondered what one looked like. Well, they reminded me of the brown dried pears of my childhood, all shriveled up and some of them almost black.

"Is that the reason the ancient Egyptians believed that gods had black skin?" I said to Betty. So many drawings or statues we had seen in the last week pertaining to the ancient gods of Egypt showed them with ebony black skin.

"Probably. You see black is the color of rebirth and identified the person as having entered the land of death and afterlife," Betty said.

I stood for a long time beside the mummy of Seti I

78

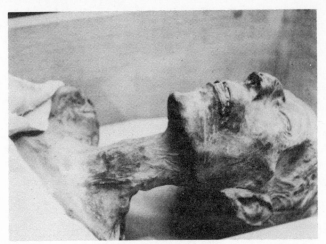

Mummy of Rameses II.

King Tutankhamun's solid gold funerary mask.

and looked into the stern lines of his dried-up dark face. Poor Seti! He tried so hard to keep his memory alive forever. He succeeded better than he bargained for. It's not his elaborate grave his forty thousand slaves built, or his well-preserved mummy which made him a household word in many places. Two chapters in the Old Testament did it for him!

"Now a new king arose over Egypt, who did not know Joseph" (Exodus 1:8; read chapters 1 and 2).

I looked for the mummy of Rameses II but the place marked with his name was empty. Betty had seen him on previous visits and had color slides of him. On our way out I found some postcards which show his mummy face. I was amazed how much alike father and son looked. How different their fame and memory could have been if they would have opened their hearts to the great God of Isaac, Jacob and Joseph!

The largest part of the second floor of the Cairo Museum has been reserved for King Tut's treasures. It took Howard Carter six years to remove, record and restore Tut's grave treasures. He found more than two thousand items. The mummy itself was never removed but left in the last of the eight shells in his tomb because the body was not too well preserved any more.

Betty and I walked from room to room and realized that the exhibition can hardly begin to show the real thing. One wonders if boy king Tut was buried with such splendor, in an unfinished small tomb, what must have been contained in Seti's or Rameses' tombs? Rameses II had a reign of sixty-six years and no other aim but to glorify himself.

The Cairo Museum contains fabulous wealth and treasures. It's overwhelming—but it depressed me. We had to leave because our time ran out, and I was glad. "Betty," I said, while we picked out postcards and some books in English to take home, "why do I feel so down? From day to day I have sensed a dull sadness grow in me that is hard to shake. It began that evening after the Sound and Light program and I have felt more and more gloomy as time goes by."

"I'm glad to hear you say that," Betty said soberly. "I always feel that way when I visit Egypt. To me Egypt is one great monument to death and it preoccupies all living and thinking."

"It preoccupied the ancient civilizations," I agreed. "But why is this kind of oppression on us in modern Egypt? The people don't believe any more as they did thousands of years ago—most of them are Moslem now."

"It's a different kind of religion here in Egypt than they have in other Islamic countries," Betty said. "I am sorry that I couldn't show you the modern City of the Dead here in present-day Cairo. I asked the guide several times to take us there but he just wouldn't do it. He even told some of the most outrageous lies to avoid it. I have no idea why he balked. You see, the Egyptians of today are still preparing themselves a house of the dead. On my last visit our guide proudly showed us his house where he and his wife will someday be buried. It was furnished, had a refrigerator and included a small room on the upper level so the children could come and visit them. The houses where the dead live are fancier than the homes they live in while they are still alive. In order to protect what they prepare for all their lives, they permit poor people to live in the houses and take care of them."

"So the City of the Dead gives at least shelter to many poor people who are still alive?" I asked.

We couldn't continue our conversation because our driver appeared with a friendly smile and with his worry beads clutched tightly in his hand. We smiled, too, and followed him to the car. Our host and guide waited and told us to hurry.

"I have another appointment with a German lady," I reminded them.

"And Hansi *must* eat something before we leave for the airport," Betty said firmly.

The two Egyptians had another argument in the Arabic language. Our host mentioned the Coptic Museum several times. He was determined to take us there yet. Our Moslem guide had something else in mind.

When we walked into the hotel, the gentlemen who had arranged the TV interview waited for us with a smartly-dressed slim lady with blond hair and blue eyes at his side.

She and I greeted each other in German and found out within the first few minutes that we were born in the same German area of Czechoslovakia. We liked each other from the beginning and began to chatter. The guide sat at the next table and acted very unhappy. He finally came over and said, "Can you please speed up your interview, we will be late."

I gave him one long cool look and said, "Our plane leaves this afternoon. I shall eat a decent lunch and *not* go *any* place, for I wish to talk to this lady."

He must have realized that he had finally pushed me too far. So he went back to his table and sulked.

My German friend recorded an interview for her

international program using her cassette recorder. And then I said in German, "I have so many un-answered questions about modern Egypt and nobody is willing to answer them. Could you give me some answers?"

"Ask," she nodded. "I'll try my best."

"Let's talk in German," I requested. I took a deep breath. "Your big dam seems to be a thing of great controversy. What do you think about it?"

"It's a mess," she said and rolled her eyes. "And since the Russians left, it has become a tragedy. Whenever anything breaks down we have no spare parts and the Russians will not readily repair things. So we have not even enough electricity from the dam any more."

"Is *that* the reason we saw only *two* turbines work-ing?" I said and winked at Betty. I couldn't wait to share our German conversation with her.

"Most likely," she said. "Things are deteriorating up there."

"Now, for my next big question," I said, "and I don't know if you will answer it. Nobody else is willing to discuss it. Why did Sadat kick the Russians out?"

"Well," she said, "the first reason is the dam. It turned out to be a mess and it's causing enough problems that someone has to take the blame, and the Russians designed and built it. But there is a much deeper cause. Sadat hates the Russians personally. He has a very unusual background. He comes from a poor peasant home and he is a self-made man. Nobody thought of him as anything special, even when he finally ended up being the vice president to Nasser."

I interrupted her and said, "I know that much. My

83

host told me that the Egyptians laughed when Sadat came into power. They said, 'We have now a mute man on top of the government, he will not last more than two weeks.' "

My German friend nodded, "Yes, Sadat surprised everybody. He kept his mouth closed while Nasser dictated, and stayed in his good graces. Nearly everyone else's head rolled. But he watched and observed and when Nasser died, Sadat took hold and established himself as a man to be reckoned with. The Russians found it out too late.

"Sadat visited Moscow on a goodwill tour while Nasser was still alive. The Russians thought of him what everybody else thought too—Sadat was a mediocre nobody. So they did not give him a reception but brushed him off at the airport. Sadat has never forgotten nor forgiven. You see, it's the worst fate that can happen to a man of the Orient or Middle East to lose face. Sadat might never say so, but the Russians humiliated him."

I nodded while new light turned on in my puzzled thinking. "Is that the reason why people here can say small or outrageous lies whenever they see fit?" I asked the woman. "I have tried to figure out why we often get the strangest answers to our simplest questions. I can ask our guide why we can't see such and such a place and he will tell us it's many kilometers away. But Betty knows very well that it is very near. I can ask our host why he isn't taking us to the place he promised and he says because his driver has to go home for evening prayer. I ask the waiter if they really have artichokes and he says, 'Yes, madam,' and then he brings us peas and carrots without blinking an eye."

My German friend laughed. "That is good observation for someone who only spent a week in Egypt. It took me much longer to learn not to take anyone's word too seriously in this culture. Truth is *never* the first option in this land. Keeping face is the most important rule of life for any Arab man."

"Well," I said, "how will that affect the talks between Sadat and our American president? Does Sadat mean what he says?"

"The Egyptians are in great hope that Carter and Sadat will understand each other because they are both farm boys," she said. "And the people here *want* peace. They are tired of wars, especially of losing them. It's too bad that the American press is giving the impression that peace can be worked out within a few weeks. How could that be? It's a deep, deep conflict that has existed since ancient times. You Americans should know best that it takes many months to work things out. It took you three years to settle the Vietnam conflict."

"You are right," I said. "But do you feel that Sadat is really going after peace, or is he trying for airplanes and weapons?"

She shrugged her shoulders. "Sadat is in a very tight spot. His personal deep hate toward the Russians is harming Egypt because the dam breaks down more and more often and the Russians are reluctant to supply the parts or technology we need to keep it repaired. His hate also leaves us without any support. The only way to get support from America is to be friendly with Israel, isn't it? Sadat and his wife are trying desperately hard to adapt this land to a Western way of life, but I don't think it can work."

85

"Why not?" I asked.

"Sadat wants to give Egypt freedom and make it a democracy but the people are not ready for it. I don't need to explain to you how democracy works. People need to be trained and prepared for such a government and if they don't know how such political freedom works, they misuse it.

"The common peasants of Egypt loved Nasser. He brought equality to the land—he made all of us equally poor. I have been living here for the last twenty years because I married an Egyptian man, and I have seen this land become desperately poor. But the peasants got a little bit of help from Nasser, so they loved him. He also set up schools and some public services.

"Sadat is trying to help the poor people too, and so is his wife. But by now we have two social classes forming. Some people have gathered wealth again and you can see many cars on the roads. Under Nasser we had no traffic jams as we have now. But the poor people are poorer than ever. So everybody is trying to get something for himself and graft, deceit and racketeering undermine the order of the land. I have no doubt that the next regime will *have* to be a dictatorship again. The people demand it for they don't know how to handle freedom. Unfortunately it's usually us, the middle class, who lose everything we have to lose," she sighed.

I sighed, too. It was time for us to leave for the airport and I had another hundred questions I wanted to ask. I thanked my new friend warmly for her willingness to answer and explain, and I promised to spend some time with her if I ever returned to Cairo.

Our limousine waited and the luggage was loaded. Our little driver pulled out swiftly and Betty and I settled back in the seat. We had driven to and from the airport several times and didn't expect any new sights—until Betty nudged me.

"Guess what?" she murmured quietly, "Our little driver friend understands more English than we gave him credit for. We are going a different way to the airport. He is driving us past the modern City of the Dead."

"Bless his heart," I grinned. "He must like us and the guide and host are so busy arguing they don't even catch on!"

We drove past a long wall where, on the other side, stood thousands of houses side by side, some small, some rather fancy: houses for the dead.

I looked quietly out of the car window and again a sentence began to repeat itself: "Here man *thought* that death was vanquished!"

"Good-bye, Egypt," I said to myself. "Good-bye and good luck. May God be merciful to you if Sadat doesn't mean what he says. May you not end up where Germany did—I pray!"

January 30—
Monday, Late Afternoon

The only way we could get from Egypt into Israel was to fly first to Jordan and then cross over the Jordanian borderline by vehicle or by foot. We flew into Amman and spent two days sight-seeing. We

City of the Dead in Cairo Egypt.

Treasury building carved out of solid rock in Petra.

visited Mount Nebo and Petra, two places I had wanted to see for a long time.

Jordan will not let tourists pass through their land unless they stay at least two days. It helps Jordan's sagging tourist industry. Before Jordan opened the border to Israel, tourists had to fly back out to a neutral point like Cypress or Greece before they could enter Israel. I was so glad we didn't have to waste extra time doing that.

But crossing into Israel from Jordan is still something else, I found out. Betty had warned me to prepare myself for stiff security measures and perhaps a walk across the little Jordan bridge. The borderline goes across the middle of the river and when she last crossed it the Jordanian guide carried her luggage to the middle point. An Israeli man carried it the other half to the other side of the Jordan bank where a tourist bus received her group and took them on their way.

This time the Jordanian bus drove all the way across to an Israeli bus terminal. We foreign visitors stayed on the bus until last. The Jordanians got out first and lined up with their bundles and suitcases for security check.

We got to the international checkpoint and found an American tour group ahead of us. So we settled down for a long wait. It took hours before we were cleared. American tourists have much in their luggage and the Jewish border guards took everything out, piece by piece, for everyone in their group. They opened every little container, unscrewed fountain pens and x-rayed every shoe. They asked the visitors to point their cameras to the ceiling and snap a picture, play their cassette recorders and run their movie cameras. It was obvious that the Israelis were not willing to take *any* chances whatsoever. They were cordial and pleasant and signs on the wall in English apologized for the inconvenience. But it had to be done for everyone's safety.

When it was finally our turn we had observed long enough to know which official to pick. One among the bunch seemed a bit more lenient and trusting than the rest. He also talked more with the visitors.

We shoved our open suitcase toward him. "Are you with the tour group?" he asked

"No," we said. "We are just the two of us."

"Where are you from?" he smiled.

"From California," we smiled back.

"What are you doing for a living?" he asked next.

"We are teachers who give lectures across America," Betty said.

"What university did you attend?" he said with an obvious interest.

"The University of Southern California," Betty smiled.

"I am a university professor myself and teach at the Hebrew University part-time," the man said while touching our stuff superficially. He took nothing out.

I unzipped the clothing bag and said, "Sir, the shoes are in here."

"Oh, thank you," he said. "I would have forgotten about it."

"Why do you x-ray every shoe?" I asked.

"We have found that Arabs have smuggled explosive devices into Israel in the hollow high heels of their shoes," the man said with a tired smile. "We cannot afford to let anything go through that could hurt either you visitors or our people."

"How tragic that there must be so much hate between races and people," I said quietly.

He nodded. "It's only very few who do the dirty work anywhere in the world. But because of the few, the rest of us must carry many extra burdens."

Our shoes had returned from the x-ray machine and he waved us through. He didn't check our handbags at all. We thanked him and wished him a good day. I didn't envy him his job. It must be hard to act the role of the suspicious bad wolf the whole day long when one has as warm and friendly a smile as that Jewish professor had.

A car and driver from our travel agency waited to take us to Jerusalem.

"Look at the difference between the Arab land and Israel," Betty said. "Wherever the Jews live it is cultivated by modern ways and is deep green. The Arabs still do it the ancient way."

The highway took us first through the Jordan valley and Jericho and then up the old caravan road through the Judean wilderness. It seemed that good rains had moistened the desert before we arrived. Wild flowers covered big patches of the rocky ground.

"One wouldn't come to Israel for the sake of breathtaking beauty of nature," I said to Betty as I looked out of the car window. "The land is mostly rocky ground, bare brown hills and simple villages—nothing spectacular like Switzerland or dainty like Holland."

Betty nodded. "This land grows on you. The more often you come here, the more of the hidden beauty you will find and the deeper you will love the land."

I smiled at her. Betty has been in Israel at least seven times in the last twelve years. She came the first time in 1966 before the Six-Day War united Jerusalem and she has watched Israel develop for the last decade.

This was only my second visit to the land of Israel but I could already understand what she was trying to say. There is something about the land of Israel that makes every Christian heart beat just a bit faster as one enters. It's almost like a burden is lifted. At least I felt a sense of relief and deep excitment spread in my soul when we finally neared Jerusalem.

Jerusalem, the Holy City! Once when I was young, deceived and brainwashed by German Nazi educators I had fallen in love with another city, Prague. We called it *Die Goldene Stadt* (the Golden City) and we Czechoslovakian young people loved her fiercely. When the war ended I had to leave, not knowing that I was never to return to her. Homesickness for that city dogged my footsteps for years and I promised myself that I would never fall in love with any place or any ideology again—or a leader, or a land, or anything, ever. The price was too high, the hurt too deep when I found out that the young idealist had been misled, and love had betrayed.

Time heals wounds and I learned to love and trust anew. Today I love God and His Holy Word. I love people. I love my new homeland, America. And I love life. I think I am also falling in love with a very special city too. I cannot help but love Jerusalem.

I wonder if a person would have to be born into the Hebrew race to understand fully the great yearning the Jews have always carried for their beloved city. For centuries they mourned and longed and wept to come home to her—while they wandered homeless and exiled over the face of the earth.

Now it has happened in our time, and I am so glad that I can be at least a rejoicing bystander. The Jews' homecoming has been my gain too. For they have opened their city to us Christians. They let us freely walk today where Jesus walked nearly two thousand years ago.

Jerusalem might have been a beautiful city in Solomon's or Christ's time, I wouldn't call her beautiful today. She doesn't compare to Vienna or Prague or even to some of the American cities that adorn themselves in greenery, flowers and beautiful youthful designs.

Jerusalem has the beauty of a mother who has grown silver gray and ageless and whose children have forgotten how she looked when she was young. She is dressed in simple garb but wears one golden ornament in her hair—the Dome of the Rock. She offers hospitality and warmth to those who have come to live under her wrap, either for a week or a lifetime. She loves to tell stories of ancient times and also of the present. When nobody takes time to listen to her experiences and wisdom, the stones of her foundations begin to whisper, sometimes they even shout.

Jerusalem's beauty is spiritual and one has to look with the eyes of the soul and heart to see it. But once you find it you will never lose it again, and it's the beginning of a new longing: to come back and come back again, to see more and more of her.

Jerusalem, I've come back!

January 31—
Tuesday Evening

Our tour group from the United States arrived last night, and today we had the first day of sight-seeing and fellowship together. The tour leader is an evangelical minister and a very dear friend of mine. His wife has never been in the Holy Land before. He is most eager to share with her what he saw on his previous visit several years ago.

Our bus driver is Samuel, a jovial elderly Jew with a pleasingly-plump waistline and a broad warm face and smile. David is slenderly built with just as friendly a disposition as Samuel. David is our tour guide.

The seventeen group members have been joined by several extra sightseers who came here to attend the International Peace Congress. Betty and I intend to take some of the congress meetings in, but we plan to spend the bulk of our time with the tour group.

I felt so sorry for the people when we loaded the bus this morning. Jet lag is a rough thing to overcome in twelve hours. Some of them looked rather dazed and bleary-eyed.

David is a good, experienced tour guide. He didn't let anyone go to sleep. His booming voice explained and pointed out continually. He also made us get out of the bus several times and walk.

We toured the old city and began near the Hill of Bad Counsel. According to Christian tradition Judas met the Sanhedrin on this hill and offered to betray Jesus Christ to them. The United Nations now has their headquarters here. I wonder if it is more than an accident that the United Nations Council would build their place on the Hill of Bad Counsel—or is it symbolic? Ever since my last world tour in 1974 I have my own convictions on that organization and I am afraid it is not the best. (See *Outposts of Love:* Old Tappan, NJ: Fleming H. Revell Company 1976.)

Well, that's how the sight-seeing started, but it got better as the day went by. Samuel skillfully drove the big bus down to the valley. It took some doing to get the big vehicle around those tight hairpin curves but he managed just fine, while some squeamish ladies squealed.

Betty pointed some of the things out that David didn't. There is the Field of Blood right below the Hill of Bad Counsel. This is the field that was bought with the thirty pieces of silver Judas threw at the chief priests' feet.

We entered the city through the Dung Gate and walked to the Wailing Wall. David called it the Western Wall. It is actually part of the retaining wall of the former temple area—all that is left of Herod's Temple.

The Jews have a legend how that small part of their Temple still remains. When Titus destroyed the Temple in A.D. 70 he gave orders not to leave one stone on top of the other but to level everything to the ground. The soldiers obeyed his orders until they came to the part which is now called the Western Wall. On this part of the wall they saw angels sitting on the top, weeping sadly. The soldiers didn't have the heart to destroy the wall below the tearful sight. Titus raged but the soldiers refused to touch the stones. Finally the general decided to start the destruction himself. He

Men's and Women's sections at Wailing Wall (Western Wall).

Hansi pointing out the prayers of Jews written on paper and put between stones in the Wailing Wall.

raised his arm—and it withered. His advisers convinced him at last to leave that small part untouched to prove that a temple had stood there and had been totally destroyed. Titus agreed and the angels wept! Their tears cemented the stones so tightly together that nobody since has been able to take them apart. Angels still weep and their tears water the tufts of grass and flower bushes that grow straight out of the wall.

Betty told this legend to some of our tour people and I looked at the bushes and remembered that two years ago we both had seen them in full bloom. They carry the delicate blossom of what we call the passionflower. The inner stamen is in the form of a cross. Parts of the flower form several nails and a crown of thorns. It is still too early in the season for many blossoms but the almond trees all over the city area are blazing with flowers.

"We can set our Jewish calendars by any wild almond tree," David said. "The blooming starts every year at the same date. We know that spring is coming when we have our yearly children's festival celebrating the almond trees' blooming. They always bloom on the *same* day."

Always on the *same* day of the Jewish year. The Jews have other festivals and worship services too, and they always gather at the wall for them. They have declared it to be an orthodox synagogue and it is by far their most reverenced spot of the nation.

Thousands throng the place on religious holidays, buses bring hundreds of worshipers to the wall every Friday before sunset. There is no better place to welcome the Sabbath. But the orthodox worshiper must hurry back and be at home before the last rays of the setting sun disappear behind the buildings of modern Jerusalem.

The orthodox Jews still try to keep the 613 commandments which the Pharisees tried to keep in Jesus' time. They walk only one-half mile on the Sabbath. They don't work; following are some examples of their definition of work on the Sabbath day:

God gave Adam the right to work and to rule and have dominion over the earth for six days. But the seventh day belongs to the Lord. So on that day, which is His day, man does not do *anything* that would show his human dominion and power over God's natural laws. That means a person cannot light a match or candle, switch on electric lights or even turn on a flash light. That would show human dominion over darkness. One cannot wash dishes or throw water on the ground. It shows power over dirt, or irrigation of the earth. (A dish can be set out into the rain and washed by nature, however.) An orthodox Jew may climb a flight of stairs by his own muscle power but he cannot use an electric elevator. He can push a door open but not walk through automatic doors. Every self-respecting Jewish hotel (like the one we stay in) has signs on their automatic entrances which read, "Sabbath entrance to the right" (or "left"), wherever the push doors are.

When Betty explained the principle to me I thought about it for a long time as we stood at the wall and watched the orthodox Jews sway in prayer chant. They have some great spiritual concepts but human nature is so prone to spoil what was defined so beautifully in the beginning. It is so right to respect God's claim on our week, but legalism can make it something unbearable, even ridiculous. An orthodox Jew cannot even comb his hair from sunset to sunset on his Sabbath because some hairs might fall out. That would be an act of reaping.

It's easy to smile about it, but are we Christians really so much above it? Haven't we spoiled, with legalism and splitting of hairs, some of the great Christian concepts which were given so perfectly to us from this great temple mount by Jesus Christ?

We climbed the temple mount and visited the Dome of the Rock. We followed the *Via Dolorosa* which means the Way of Sorrows, the way of the Cross. We stood in Pilate's judgment hall on the same pavement Jesus of Nazareth stood on nearly two thousand years ago. It was mind-boggling!

When we entered the convent of the Sisters of Zion, we were led down a stairway to the level of the city in Jesus' time. Modern Jerusalem is about ten feet higher than the ancient city was. On the old pavement ancient Roman soldiers had scratched some of their games which they used for entertainment. They are still there. David pointed at one of them called "The Game of the King." It was a game in which a convicted person was blindfolded after being dressed up like a mock king—in a robe, a crown and with a scepter. They made fun of him, tortured and hit him and demanded that he guess who struck him. The game always ended with a crucifixion. We all walked silently away. Such moments make the Bible very real—too real for comfort! (See Mark 15:16–20.)

After lunch Samuel drove us to Holy Land Hotel to see the scale model of Jerusalem during the second temple period, which is the way it looked during the time of Christ. Jerusalem must have been a beautiful city when our Lord walked in it. The white-golden Temple stood alone like a dazzling diamond on top of Mount Moriah. One ancient historian writes: "He who has not seen Herod's Temple, has never beheld beauty."

It must have been hard for Jesus' disciples to believe that such splendor and might would some day be gone. But it was destroyed, as it had been many times before. And the city was even more beautiful in Solomon's time. The first temple period superceded by far the second temple period at Christ's time.

Jerusalem has been destroyed and rebuilt thirty-two times since King David conquered Jebus or Salem. He made it his city, and so it was called the city of David or Jerusalem.

What is it that makes people feel so intense about a place like Jerusalem? They are either enemies who are determined to destroy it or friends who are willing to give their lifeblood to defend and rebuild it. What is it that Jerusalem has that other cities don't seem to have?

Jerusalem has a promise! God has promised that this city will live and be blessed by Him. This is what God's prophet Zechariah said:

> *Thus says the Lord of hosts, "I am exceedingly jealous for Zion, yes, with great wrath I am jealous for her." Thus says the Lord, "I will return to Zion and will dwell in the midst of Jerusalem. Then Jerusalem will be called the City of Truth, and the mountain of the Lord of hosts will be called the Holy Mountain." Thus says the Lord of*

hosts, *"Old men and old women will again sit in the streets of Jerusalem, each man with his staff in his hand because of age. And the streets of the city will be filled with boys and girls playing in its streets."* Thus says the Lord of hosts, *"If it is too difficult in the sight of the remnant of this people in those days, will it also be too difficult in My sight?"* declares the Lord of hosts. Thus says the Lord of hosts, *"Behold I am going to save My people from the land of the east and from the land of the west; and I will bring them back and they will live in the midst of Jerusalem, and they will be My people and I will be their God in truth and righteousness"* (Zechariah 8:2–8).

February 1— Early Wednesday Afternoon

Most of the day was filled with two long bus rides to and from Beersheba. Betty assured me that every Jewish guide insists that he take his tour group to Beersheba, a place modern Israel is immensely proud of.

Beersheba is a name well known to Old Testament readers. It is connected with Abraham, Isaac and Jacob.

Before the founding of modern Israel it was a tiny little Bedouin village, located in the middle of the desert. Jewish immigrants began to settle there and, within thirty years, it became a thriving metropolis, the capital of the Negev. It has its own university, an extensive library and various industries. David, our guide, pointed at the unusual forms of the modern public buildings and the rows of apartment houses.

"We are experimenting with new designs to combat the problems of desert living," he said. "This city often faces sandstorms that darken the noonday sun. It also reaches summer temperatures of up to 140 degrees or more. So the people who live here must learn to protect themselves against the sand in the air and excessive heat. Most buildings are constructed of heavy cement. If they have any windows they are set in deep and are very slim. The library has no windows; it is lit entirely by artificial light."

We ate in the dining room of a large hotel and I enjoyed the crisp salads and vegetables they served with the main course. It is absolutely safe to eat raw salads in Israel and one can also drink the water in Jewish establishments. The Jews are sticklers for cleanliness and have very strict food laws. They also observe kosher eating rules and a visitor would have to go far to find any pork. They never serve dairy products and meat at the same meal. Not only that but they even serve the meals on different dishes. Our hotel in Jerusalem served breakfast on china with a black trim and dinner on plates with a red trim.

Breakfast is a feast, served smorgasbord style. Fresh vegetables like grated raw carrots, sweet cucumbers, crisp greens, pickled red beets and various other raw foods are laid out with cheese, yogurt, smoked or pickled fish, eggs and milk. Coffee and tea are served by the waiters. No meat is served until the next meal when no cheese and milk are offered. The Jews try to

102

obey their cultural rules even if they don't adhere to the ultra-orthodox way of the Hassidim, the group who dresses in the long black robes, fur hats and with their hair and beard in ringlets.

Even the non-religious Jew will attend services on the Jewish New Year and go to the synagogue on the Day of Atonement. They call it Yom Kippur and it's observed world-wide by the Jewish race.

I asked Samuel about it. He and I had become good friends. His parents came from Poland and he was three years old when they entered *eretz Israel,* long before the state of Israel was recognized by the world.

"I don't go often to the synagogue, little one," he said, "I must work and the weekend is usually when I drive the bus for tourists. But I fulfill my obligations and will never work on Yom Kippur."

I understood why he and David had to work so hard. I still remember when at my last visit our Jewish guide said to me, "We pay a *very* high price for the privilege of living in this, our land. Our taxes are often as high as 75 percent of our entire income. Most of the money goes into the defense budget. Every Israeli lives like the people of Nehemiah's time—we carry a work shovel in one hand and a sword in the other!"

Only Jews pay taxes and serve in the army, both men and women alike. Arabs live tax free in Israel and are exempt from army service, but they receive government aid for their children and free medical care. Basic schooling is provided for every child in Israel, including the Arab children who are taught in their own language.

The whole state of Israel has around three and one-half million citizens; three million are Jews, the rest are Arabs. That does not include the occupied territory Israel oversees such as the West Bank and the area directly south of Jerusalem which was, like the old city, part of Jordan until the Six-Day War in 1967. Arabs are the main population in such places.

We drove through the Arab towns and cities on the way to Beersheba. Samuel stopped for us in Hebron and David led us into the mosque beneath which are the graves of Abraham, Isaac, Jacob, Sarah, Rebecca and Leah. (Rachel is buried near Bethlehem.)

I was surprised that we were permitted to get out of the bus in Hebron. The last time we only stopped and the people took pictures through the bus windows. Betty voiced her surprise too.

Hebron is one of Israel's trouble spots and Arabic unrest often starts in that place. One of the reasons for the tensions between the two races is the grave of their common father, Abraham. The Moslem Arabs guarded his grave with great jealousy and Jews were not allowed inside the mosque even during Palestinian days. After the Six-Day War the Jews became the rulers and opened the mosque to the public, Jews and Gentiles alike. They even made one small room near the grave into a synagogue. It makes the Arabs' blood boil.

We had no problems and everything appeared rather peaceful. I looked around and nudged Betty quietly. On top of a house right across from the place we visited stood several Jewish soldiers with guns in their hands. One of our American tourist ladies saw them too. And as we stood together while David was explaining something, she interrupted him and said, "David, why are your soldiers stationed everywhere carrying guns and machine guns? We saw them all over Bethlehem, even at the Church of the Nativity. (It is built over the cave where Jesus Christ was supposedly born.) They were in the old city of Jerusalem, I see them here in Hebron. Sometimes they are even in the middle of a road with road blocks. Why must you have all these soldiers running around? I thought you had *peace* in the Middle East right now!"

David smiled and give a little sigh. "It is hard to explain to an American that the rest of the world does not live like America does. The rest of the world does not even *think* like Americans do. Your concept of peace is something that nobody else has, not even the Europeans. Your country has forgotten what it is to live with war and in a post-war period. The Middle East never has. Peace for us means to live without war for a few years, maybe five, maybe ten or even twenty years. If you read the Old Testament you will find that the history of this land knows nothing but war; peace is mixed into it a few years at a time. The longest period of peace existed under Solomon. There was peace for one whole generation—forty years. It is a way of life for us to be thankful for every single year of peace we have.

"Israel became an independent state in 1948. Since then we have had four wars. We are surrounded by forty million Arabs who want to drive us Jews into the sea.

"So, today the sun is shining and we have no war. We don't think too far ahead, but we are glad for every day God gives us life!"

Nobody said anything after David's little speech. I had a big lump in my throat.

Yes, I have become an American, too. I had forgotten what it meant to live with short years of uneasy peace between wars like the rest of the world does. I also had begun to take for granted the privilege I have of living in America during a century of peace. It's so *easy* to forget how the rest of the world has to live—not by choice but of necessity!

I smiled at some Jewish soldiers when we passed them to board the bus and I said, "Shalom." They didn't smile back. Jewish soldiers take their jobs seriously. They don't smile or chat when on duty. They just stand and watch. They watch friend and foe ever so carefully!

"It's actually a miracle that three million Jews can survive when surrounded by so much hostility and overshadowed by Russia," I said quietly to Betty. "I admire their spirit and courage with all my heart."

"So do I," Betty said. "I have loved and respected them for a long time. When I visited Israel after the Six-Day War and we stayed in an Arab hotel, I was talking to the man at the desk about the changes in the city after the last war. I finally said to him, 'How do you explain that three million Jews could resist and conquer forty million Arabs and win this war?'

"The man looked at me without a smile and said, 'We can take care of the Jews. It's their God we cannot handle.' "

It is good to have the God of Abraham, Isaac and Jacob on one's side. He always keeps His promises. He promised the Jews that they would be gathered again in the land of their fathers before the end of time. They gathered! He promised them that He would make their desert bloom. The desert is blooming! He promised them prosperity if they would keep His law. The land is prospering! The only great void in their land and life is the Messiah who hasn't come yet. God said that someday He will open their eyes and they will see—Him!

February 2—
Late Thursday Afternoon

This is our "free" day and everybody does as he or she pleases. Betty and I took a taxi to the old city and did some shopping, the rest of the day we just relaxed and talked. We had a lot to talk about. We went last night to hear Prime Minister Begin speak at the Peace Conference.

That evening was another event which will influence my thinking for the rest of my life, I am sure.

First of all, I had to change my mental picture about Begin. Through our American press I had received the idea that he was a hard man, stubborn, obstinate and unwilling to yield to sensible suggestions. A hard-liner of the old school who doesn't care if the world blows up as long as he and Israel have their way.

He isn't that way at all. When he walked in last night, surrounded by security men, he appeared weary, his shoulders stooped a bit. He was late and the audience sang to pass the time. It just so happened that we were singing the little round called, "Shalom" when he entered. We kept on singing while we stood to welcome him. The place was packed with evangelical

Christians from eight countries. But the bulk were from the United States.

Begin is a soft-spoken man who looks through dark-rimmed glasses with warm eyes; he has a shy, gentle smile.

It's hard to picture him as a leading member, perhaps one who played a decisive role in the Irgun, the underground organization that fought the British in Palestine. He was described by them as a brute, a murderer and a heartless man.

Betty bought Begin's book today. It is called *The Revolt (Menachem Begin,* published by Stern Matzky's Agency, Ltd, P.O. Box 628, Tel Aviv, 1952, 1972, 1977).

After seeing and hearing him that night, I began to understand why an English editor wrote in the preface of the book:

> *Historical irony chose one of the gentlest, kindest, most selfless of men to lead a rebellion against stupendous odds, and to dominate the forces which he led by the sheer strength of his moral influence. That he should have been cast by his opponents in the role of an ogre of all iniquities is merely another example of human stupidity, "with which," as Schiller so truly wrote, "the gods themselves struggle in vain." (Ivan M. Greenberg, London, March 1951.)*

The prime minister sounded weary and sometimes his tired voice broke when he spoke about the suffering of his generation. I sat and listened and let my tears roll. Yes, it was my race that caused so much of that suffering. How can the world forget so fast how *much* the Jews have suffered in our time?

I wasn't the only one who cried. His speech got to the heart of many listeners. At the end we stood for a standing ovation. He had to leave for another meeting before our evening program closed and we were asked not to leave our seats while he walked out. We understood. Security was tight.

As he came down from the podium, the audience began spontaneously to sing the little song "Shalom" again. It moved the prime minister visibly. He broke through the circle of his security men and began to shake hands with the audience. As many hands as he could get to, he would shake and say over and over: "God bless you! Thank you for coming! Please, enjoy your stay!"

We sang Shalom until he had left the auditorium. I was told this morning that Begin supposedly turned to one of his security men while he rushed on to another meeting and said: "I have never felt more weary than when I came to this meeting. I have never been so refreshed in such a short time as tonight. They gave me so much love and friendship."

Betty and I prayed for that burdened and tired man last night and we prayed for him this morning. We intend to keep on praying for him. Just as I pray for Sadat and our American president, Jimmy Carter. They all need our prayers and love, not our criticism.

Here are some excerpts of the speech I shall never forget:

There are some people, wise, learned, even sophisti-cated who accuse me that I am founding our rights to

109

this land on the Bible. What an accusation! I plead guilty! And I don't apologize.

Yes indeed, my dear friends, the heart of every man of good will is uplifted when he remembers that four thousand years ago, at the dawn of human civilization, the words were uttered to the father of our nation, Abraham: "Unto thy seed I will give this land." And the prophet Ezekiel said, "And they shall know that I am the Lord when I shall bring you into the land of Israel, into the country for which I lifted up My hand to give it to your fathers." And when our people were exiled for seventy years to the banks of the rivers of Babylon, they gave an oath: "If I forget thee, O Jerusalem, let my right hand forget her cunning." And when the Romans launched their ultimate attack upon the temple mountain—the fifth and the twelfth legion—and the Temple was set ablaze and the people were subjugated and the country destroyed, our forefathers, hearing the Roman legionnaires saying, "Judea is defeated; Judea is captured," repeated that oath of the banks of the rivers of Babylon; again, generations ago, when our people went into exile, were dispersed and humiliated and persecuted and ultimately physically destroyed.

And yet, by the order of Divine Providence, ladies and gentlemen, we are again in Jerusalem. And we can say that Jerusalem is not defeated, neither captured, but resurrected.

It is a unique event in the annals of mankind, never witnessed, never seen after nineteen centuries of all that happened to our people, and especially in our generation, [that] we have in the land of Israel, in its capital city—eternal, reunited, indivisible—this joyous meeting of our friends. Isn't it a proof of Divine Providence, of

110

ways we cannot even know in advance? We can only see post factum how Divine Providence works. He performs miracles indeed and then gives victory to a just cause.

My dear friends, yes, indeed, our ancient people gave eternal life to the Book and the Bible gave eternal life to our people. So we indeed found our right on the Bible, on the vision, on the pledge, on all that is sacred to the Jews and to the Christians, to all men of faith and good will.

Then, also, the fact that our generation is almost a biblical generation, I say so with deep respect and a measure of hesitation. [We are] no comparison to our forefathers. I would be blasphemous to make such a comparison. What was that generation which left the house of Egypt, went through the desert for forty years with all the difficulties and crises and the attacks and the fights, and ultimately reached this little country, this little piece of land, with which we are bound forever to be on and together? What was the story or the history of that generation? Everything was in suffering! And everything was achieved in heroism. What suffering! And what heroism!

Now comes our generation. The suffering that was the portion of my generation is indescribable. My dear friends, let us remember those days. Every day twelve thousand of our brethren rode to their wanton death in the gas chambers—day in, day out, night in, night out. The world knew; the world was indifferent. Nobody came to their rescue. They cried out from the depths, "Help us! Save us!" They were alone.

Every day twelve thousand people, amongst them little children and babies torn away from the arms of their parents, rode to those gas chambers—in the heart

111

of Europe, when a great nation calling itself for centuries the nation of philosophers, thinkers and poets was turned into a bloodthirsty mob by what Churchill termed, "all the embodiment of evil in mankind." And the most horrendous atrocities ever perpetrated on earth since God created the world and men made themselves Satan. Such atrocities have never been perpetrated scientifically, methodically, day in, day out, year in, year out, to destroy a whole people. A million and a half of our little children.

My dear friends, that has been our suffering. Unheard of, for the first time in the annals of mankind. The people suffered so much. And those who survived the holocaust, the remnants of our people, had to witness what happened to their mothers and their fathers and their little nephews—all the families—and to the great brains, and to the poor one. Six million! A third!

My dear friends, in terms of the American people that meant the destruction of eighty million men and women. Eighty million! This is our portion. That was the chapter of suffering.

There is also the heroism. With the last vestige of our national strength, having lost a third of our people, the best of our young men, we rose in revolt against this intolerable fate of our people. To be disbursed, not to have a flag, no means of self-defense, to be humiliated, landless and then to see the ultimate fate. We revolted against it.

It cannot go on like this. We had a country; we were thrown out by force from it. We shall go back! We will not take away anything from anybody; [this] is the land of our forefathers where we built our civilization, where our kings knelt to the Almighty, and the prophets

112

brought forth that vision of eternal peace in which we believe with all our hearts: "And they shall beat their swords into plowshares, their spears into pruning hooks, nation shall not lift up sword against nation, neither shall they learn war any more."

This is the land. Now we want to come back to it, till it, make it green again, work on it [and], if necessary, defend it. Therefore we fought—the few against the many—with God's help! As it happened several times in the history of our nation, the few won the day. And we raised our flag among the flags of free and independent nations thirty years ago. And we built up this land. Many of you visited it many times, you have seen the changes. How green now are our valleys, all the valleys.

I remember when we went from Tel Aviv to Jerusalem in 1967 after its liberation. On both sides [the land] was completely gray. Now, bless His Name, it is green because our people love this land and therefore they till it and work on it and make it flourishing. And they plant trees—now you can see [them] in every corner, in every part of the land after centuries of being completely abandoned.

Now, ladies and gentlemen, we yearn for peace and pray for peace. It is so natural; so self-understood. We lost so much. Our generation lived through ten wars, amongst them two world wars. In this country eleven times we had to save our very existence from attacks. Eleven times! In the last thirty years we had to wage five wars, again to save our people from the danger of utter destruction. Always attacked, ambushed, our blood shed, threatened, "Throw them into the sea, destroy them."

Therefore we dream about peace. We pray for it every

*minute of our lives. It has been denied to us. For the last
thirty years we did not have one day of peace. Until the
Six-Day War there were the so-called demarcation
lines, completely indefensible, invasions which were
impossible to stop. We lost thousands of our people.
Again men, women and children being killed and
maimed. Now, we want peace!*

*Therefore, when President Sadat made his first state-
ment to the People's Council in Cairo that he is ready to
come to the Knesset, the following day I invited him,
"Please do come," although between the two countries
there was a state of war proclaimed—not by us, by the
other side. He put out two demands: total withdrawal to
those indefensible, breakable lines; and the [founding of
the] so-called Palestine state in Judea, Samaria and
Gaza, which would in no time turn into a big central
Soviet base in the Middle East with all the modern
sophisticated weapons which the Soviet Union was able
through an airlift to bring to faraway countries—An-
gola, Mozambique, Ethiopia, Southern Yemen, with the
Paraguayan revolutionaries, the Cubans—exporting
communism to the four corners of the world. From
Odessa to Judea to Bethlehem is only a matter of a flight
of two hours. Two hours on a cargo, supersonic jet plane
which the Russians have in numbers. That would be a
mortal danger to us, a great peril to the free world. From
this piece of land [which Sadat wants us to surrender],
you can go northwards, eastwards, southwards—in all
directions of the Middle East. Saudi Arabia is around
the corner, indeed, and there is some coveting of what is
there beneath the surface.*

*Ladies and gentlemen, it is so obvious, so clear, the
whole civilian population of Israel would be within the*

114

*range of conventional artillery. Soviet artillery is now
within the range of 43.8 kilometers. We would be nine
miles from the seashore, at the most twenty miles—
between nine and twenty miles. Every city, town and
village would be in the range of conventional Soviet
guns supplied in the hundreds, perhaps thousands, to the
most implacable enemy of our people since the days of
the Nazis, [who stated] in writing that the State of Israel
must disappear, be wiped off the map.*

*Can we, should we place again our men, women and
children in the range of our enemies' fire? So that they
would be daily in danger and any minute can fall? Can
we allow that Jerusalem be again encircled in cross fire
from the north, El Bireh and from the south, Bethlehem? A few miles! Can we again place our parliament,
the heart of our democracy, in the range of simple
mortars as was the case only eleven years ago when from
the hills of Bethlehem, the Knesset was shelled by
conventional mortars? Can we bring upon our women
and children this danger again from which we extricated
ourselves with the sacrifices of our best men and [be]
threatened time and again with extinction? I put [to you]
these questions. They are not rhetorical questions,
everybody can answer them. I know what is your answer
in your hearts.*

*Now, my dear friends, we started to negotiate peace
and we want to continue these negotiations. What we
said is as simple as this: Everything is negotiable, except
the destruction of Israel!*

*When two such ultimate plans are put to us—total
withdrawal, relinquishing Judea, Samaria, Gaza, descending from the Golan Heights, putting again all the
valley within the range of simple machine guns, as we*

have experienced for nineteen years, and then restore the situation in which we faced daily the danger of being destroyed—that no man or woman of good will will ever advise us to do. We want peace. We yearn for it. We pray for it. We want to negotiate it. But there must be real peace. In other words, peace with security for our people.

On the other hand, we want to live with our neighbors, our Arab neighbors, in human dignity, in equality of rights, in justice, in advancement. And therefore we made a proposal for the first time in the history of the Palestinian Arabs. We offered ministerial autonomy, complete autonomy, unlimited autonomy. They will elect for themselves an eleven-member council. That council will have eleven departments covering all spheres of daily life and administrations—agriculture and industry and religious affairs and education—all spheres of life. We will not interfere in their life what-soever. Only what do we ask as a result of experience? As a result of a logical analysis of the great possibilities? Security! Then the Palestinian Arabs will have auton-omy, the Palestinian Jews will have security. This is the fairness of our proposal.

And when I brought our peace proposal in two parts— the bi-lateral Egyptian/Israeli relations and the auton-omy for the Palestinian Arabs—to the president of the United States, the secretary of state, ranking senators, former president Gerald Ford, all of them had words of praise for this peace plan of Israel. It is decent, it is fair, it is far-reaching, it is sweeping because we want peace. There is now a propaganda campaign launched to prove that what is good is bad, day is night. The ancient sophists tried to do so. But we are simple men. What is, as President Carter says, "a long step forward," cannot become in five weeks "a short step backwards." What was a notable contribution cannot become, by a whim, negativism.

So we believe men and women of good will will go on supporting, throughout the free world, our peace plan with its fairness and decency. And we are prepared, of course, to negotiate on the basis of complete equality— no victors, no vanquished, equals sit around the table and look together for a solution. We will do so. A solution will be found, peace will come, peace treaties will be concluded and signed, and a new era, a God-blessed era, will start in the cradle of the civilization which is the Middle East.

Ladies and gentlemen, on behalf of the government of Israel and the people, may I thank you, all our friends for your friendship, for your help, understanding. How good it is to be among friends. I know that you are friends of Israel in your hearts, in your faith, in your souls. That you pray together with us for the liberty and for the justice which our generation must leave to our children and children's children. And because you are just and righteous women and men, you pray for Israel and Israel's future. We are grateful to you.

We greet you tonight in Jerusalem and in Israel and we know that you will tell your friends all over the United States, all over the world, "Israel deserves our friendship and our help." Let us stand together. Look, my dear friends, the free world has been shrinking. It became an island battered by high seas and waves. Look what is happening in Europe and in Africa and in Asia, how serfdom tries to take over country after country.

There is only one condition that liberty can have

success: If all free women and men stand together and defend all the values which make life worthwhile to live. And therefore, on behalf of Israel, I appeal to all of you and to your friends again, let us stand together. Yes indeed, again from the prophet, we shall remember his call to the house of Jacob, "Come ye, and let us walk in the light of the Lord." Let us all walk in the light of the Lord. And with God's help, liberty and justice will win the day to live forever and ever.

When Mr. Begin finished speaking, Charles Smith, a minister in Southern California, responded with a few words:

Mr. Prime Minister, since the day that God ordained that you should lead His people in this land which He has given to you by a covenant that will never end, our prayers, our respect and admiration for you have grown. We want you to know that we stand with you and we do believe that this land is yours by God's divine right. We admire your courage and we pray that God will continue to give you that courage to stand in the midst of ungodly pressures. We would like to give to you a wall hanging which has upon it a descending dove, the universal symbol of peace. And it is our prayer that this peace will come, not only to Israel, but to the world. And we believe that this peace will surely come when the Messiah, whom the Jewish people are praying for and we also are praying for, shall come and establish this peace upon the earth. It is our conviction that when the Messiah does come, both Christian and Jew alike will find that we have been praying for the same one.

February 3—Friday Evening

This is our last night in Jerusalem. Tomorrow the bus will drive us up to Galilee and to a kibbutz at the Lebanon borderline.

We spent the biggest part of today driving down to Masada and on the way back Samuel stopped for an hour at the Dead Sea so people could swim or sunbathe.

Betty and I didn't go into the water. We just laid in the sun and talked. Ever since we heard Begin speak we have talked and talked—about the way Israel began, about the wars and other historic Israeli facts. I am rather ignorant on many happenings that other Americans know all along and perhaps take for granted.

When Israel became an independent nation in 1948 I still lived in Germany and was caught in the struggle of after-war survival as a refugee in western Germany. The Sinai campaign occurred in 1956, one year after I came to America. I didn't speak or read English well enough then to be able to read a newspaper. The first time I took an interest in Israel was at the Six-Day War in 1967. But the whole event began and ended so quickly that it didn't seem like it was that big a thing. To Betty it is obviously most important, for she dates all the stories she tells around the Six-Day War: "It happened before the Six-Day War," she will say. Or, "It happened after the Six-Day War."

The Six-Day War united Jerusalem. For the first time after nearly twenty-five hundred years the Jews were again in control of their city and their own land.

The last time it happened was before Nebuchadnezzar's siege in 592 B.C.

From 1948 until 1967 the old city belonged to Jordan, the new city was in Israel. When Betty visited Jerusalem the first time there was *no* connection between the old and new cities whatsoever—no road connections, no telephone lines, no postal service crossed the borderline, no Jew was allowed to visit the old city, not even as a tourist.

Betty and her group had started their visit to the Middle East in 1966 by flying into Jordan. They had walked through the old city and visited all the other tourist spots of Jordan. On the day they were to cross over to Israel and the new city they had to walk across the Mandelbaum Gate and carry their own luggage through no-man's-land from one border to the next, a distance of perhaps fifty yards.

Her group took a little bit more time than expected and the bus on the Israeli side had to be informed to pick them up one hour later. There was no way to get the message through to Israel from Jordan but to send a telegram to the American travel agency in Paris. They in turn notified the agency in the new city of Jerusalem and the bus arrived to pick them up. Such things can boggle the American way of thinking!

In the Six-Day War, Israel promised Jordan that they would not attack them unless Jordan attacked first. The war began with Egypt and Israel fighting each other alone. Egypt's Nasser convinced Hussein, king of Jordan, to launch a surprise attack on Israel in order to help the losing Egyptians. This gave the Israelis the chance they had been waiting for. Hussein attacked the new Jerusalem on the first day of the war.

He shelled it with mortars and rockets. The Israelis regrouped on the third day and went for the old city. They determined not to bomb—the ancient holy places had to be preserved. It would mean great sacrifice of human lives and blood, but it *had* to be—and it was!

The old city was taken mostly by hand-to-hand battle, inch by inch, meter by meter. Many lives were lost. The Israelis had a problem; they brought no maps since they had not planned on fighting with Jordan, thus there was no way to plot an attack. So they first conquered the Rockefeller Museum in which there were ancient maps of the city. The old city had not changed its face so the old maps were adequate for their needs.

Mordechai Gur, commander of the paratroop brigade, decided to charge the city from the east directly. He got permission and started to drive down the Mount of Olives. (Jewish officers don't say, "Forward march," their orders are "Follow me.") Paratroopers prepared to jump from the air while Gur was on his way to the city in his half-track. Suddenly he told his driver to stop and turn back. The historic importance of that moment had suddenly dawned on him and he decided to do it with the proper flourish.

Standing on the Mount of Olives he faced the temple mount, picked up his transmitter and flicked on the switch. Addressing the commanders of all regiments, he said, "We stand today at the gates of the old city—where so many of our dreams lie. Now we are going up to the old city, the temple mount, the wailing wall. The order of battle is as follows—" Then he gave the *actual* unit numbers and the plan of attack, breaking all rules of code and security in modern military warfare. He finished by saying: "For thousands of years the Jewish people have prayed for this moment. Israel is awaiting our victory. Good luck!"

Gur hopped back on his half-track and his driver roared down the hill. Leading the way, he urged over the radio: "Faster, boys, faster! You're making history!"

Mordechai Gur was the first Jew to enter the old city in many, many years. Several times he was asked to announce that they were in but he refused. The truck raced forward and upward to the *only* place where Gur could announce the victory. One-and-a-half hours after it all started, Gur reached for his transmitter and said: "The temple mount is in our hands. Repeat, the temple mount is in our hands!"

Betty had told me that story before but she loves to tell it over and over again. She can never tell it without her eyes misting and her voice cracking at the end. I have a similar problem when it comes to the overwhelming story of Masada.

Today I visited the Masada rock for the second time and it got to me as much as or more than the first time.

The bus took us east of Jerusalem through the Judean wilderness. We passed the Dead Sea to the eastern edge of the Jordan plateau and stopped at the foot of the mountain.

The huge rock sticks out like a natural fortress in a strange defiant way. Sheer cliffs drop on all sides. The flat top is shaped like a diamond and stands thirteen hundred feet above the Dead Sea. It is a very difficult climb to the top, but it can be done by way of the snake path on the sharp eastern slope, or from the west along

Masada showing Roman ramp with Dead Sea in background.

Israeli young people climbing the Snake Path winding past cisterns up toward Herod's hanging palace.

a spur which leads into a series of winding goat paths, or up the ramp.

We tourists did none of these. We went to the top by cable cars which were installed less than ten years ago by the Israeli government. Betty told me that she walked up the ramp the first time she visited the place in 1969 and it was hard and hot. Someday I would like to climb it by foot too. And I want to go up the eastern side.

But it is the story of the western edge that gives us lumps in our throats and burns our hearts and eyes with deep sadness. The Masada story is old and was recorded by Flavius Josephus, historic writer who lived just after the time of Christ.

Josephus was a Jew born in A.D. 37 who rose to a high position in the Jewish state and then betrayed his own people in order to save his life. He made friends with the Romans, was made a Roman citizen, awarded a pension and lived on an estate in Judea. He wrote a seven-volume history of *The Wars of the Jews with the Romans* and a two-volume account of *The Antiquities of the Jews,* as well as many other works. The only physical description of Jesus that exists comes to us from Josephus. And the only contemporary account of the awesome events that happened on and around Masada come down the ages in detailed description from his pen alone.

It wasn't until the Jewish archaeologist and professor, Yigael Yadin, one the the foremost specialists in our times on biblical archaeology in Israel, decided to prove or disprove history that we know that Josephus was correct and his story of Masada is true.

What a story! It is the heroic tale of 960 Jewish

zealots, men, women and children, who chose death rather than surrender to slavery under the Romans.

Masada began to make history ninety years before the zealots occupied it. Herod the Great, the one who is known to the Christians for his slaying of the little children in Bethlehem, made Masada a fortress and one of his palaces. He never used it as a refuge, however. He died several years after Christ's birth.

Herod was an Idumean but a strong ally and friend of the Romans. Little did he know, to use the words of Josephus, "that he was to leave it [Masada] to the Romans as their very last task in the war against the Jews."

What a task it proved to be to the invincible mighty Roman Empire!

In A.D. 66 the Jews throughout the country rose as one to drive the Romans from their land. The result is known in history as the Great Jewish War against the Romans. Rome sent her most famous general, Vespasian, to suppress the rebellion. It took him five years to do it. His son, Titus, finished the job and conquered Jerusalem after his father had to return to Rome.

The Romans figured they had subdued the land when they finally raided Jerusalem and destroyed the Jewish Temple, the holiest Jewish shrine the Jews had. Titus decided to set an example to others who might get the idea and rebel so he slaughtered thousands of Jews and took more of them to Rome to become slaves. But he didn't catch all of them. Some got away, determined to keep up their fight and resistance. They were led by Eleazar ben Yair and were called zealots. They received their name because of their "zeal for the Lord" and their "zeal for what was right!"

Eleazar and his group made their painful escape to the east of Jerusalem through the Judean desert toward Masada after Jerusalem fell. It was a long, merciless scramble through shadeless desert heat and cold nights. They had no food and very little water; sharp rocks tore their weary flesh. It must have taken them weeks to get to Masada which had been conquered by a group of zealots at the beginning of the Jewish war. The Romans hadn't bothered to retake it. They figured the Jewish resistance was over after Jerusalem fell. It wasn't!

The zealots of Masada settled in Herod's fortress prepared to hold that last fort of freedom as long as they lived. Herod had stored enough food to feed thousands of people for many years—grain does not spoil in the dry desert air, not for decades. Every drop of rain water had been gathered in deep cool cisterns so that there was enough water in reserve to meet the bathing and drinking needs of all the families. The palace buildings themselves were luxurious and despised by the frugal zealots, but they used every corner and also the double wall spaces as housing and chambers for the few hundred families who fled to Masada for refuge and shelter.

The zealots continued to stay at Masada for three years, which annoyed the Romans to no end. It was a matter of prestige and principle for Rome that Masada had to be conquered, but how?

Flavius Silva, the new procurator of Judea, decided that he himself would take care of that annoying rebels' nest. In A.D. 72 he marched the famous Tenth Legion and additional troops (from six thousand to ten thousand fighters in all) to conquer less than a thousand zealots—including women and children. What a compliment to the Jews' courageous spirit! In addition to his soldiers Silva brought fifteen thousand Jewish slaves to carry water and supplies and serve the Romans. We don't know how long it took to move such a large force to the foot of Masada, west of the Dead Sea—the lowest habitable spot on earth, twelve hundred feet below sea level.

Silva looked at the sheer cliffs and knew he couldn't storm Masada as long as the fighters on top could roll down stones or pour boiling oil upon those who tried the climb. The west side of Masada falls in a sharp angle only about one-fifth of the way. Then there is a spur, a kind of bridge, called the "white cliff" linking the rock with the flat plateau. Silva decided to attack from the west side. He built a siege wall that encircled the fortress. Behind the wall, his troops watched the fort, alert to a possible attack or escape. Then Silva's fifteen thousand slaves began building a ramp up the west side. They piled earth and stone, built wooden scaffolding to hold the earth and slowly but surely laid an approach to the fort.

The zealots stood on top of their wall and watched the ramp grow bigger and closer. Day after day, week after week for long months they watched. Did they fight the slaves who built it? We don't know. But we wonder what went on in the hearts of the men who faced each other day by day, some looking down, others looking up, knowing that all of them—defenders and slaves—were of the same blood and race: sons of Abraham.

When the ramp was completed in A.D. 73, the Roman soldiers rolled the battering-rams up the ramp

127

to destroy the walls of the fortress. But the zealots had anticipated it and built an inner wall of timber fortified with rocks and dirt.

Silva called for firebrands and commanded that torches be hurled against the wooden wall. The dry wood caught fire and soon the whole section was ablaze. Then a strange wondrous event took place, the wind changed and the fire and smoke turned toward the faces of the Roman soldiers, threatening to destroy the siege towers and battering rams.

Josephus tells that the unexpected turn of events "plunged the Romans into despair." The zealots cheered. God was on their side, they would prevail! But hope died when the wind changed again and the timber wall burned to ashes.

As night settled over the red hot embers, the Romans returned to their camp at the foot of the mountain knowing that victory would be theirs by the dawn of the next day. And the zealots knew that the moment of greatest crisis had come. They had not only come to the end of their valiant fight, they wondered why God had abandoned them. Had they not tried to fight *His* fight? Would they now have to end their heroic struggle by becoming slaves and march chainbound through Rome?

What choice did they have? They could either choose surrender—or death. Eleazar assembled his fighters and delivered one of the most moving and dramatic speeches in history. The speech has been preserved for us in the writings of Josephus.

Jews do not believe in suicide unless they have to choose between it and slavery. Death is *always* to be chosen above bondage and Eleazar delivered his plan to the men of his zealot community: "Let every man execute his own family. Let a lot choose ten men who then will execute all the men. Let a lot choose one of the ten men to kill the last nine and then fall on his own sword.

"Let us die *free* men, gloriously surrounded by our wives and children and let us be expeditious. Eternal renown shall be ours by snatching the prize from the hands of our enemies, and leaving them nothing to triumph over but the bodies of those who dared to be their own executioners."

The zealots agreed unanimously and lost no time in doing what had to be done. Josephus tells in moving words about the last moments of that grim happening.

Every head of a household embraced his wife and children tenderly for the last time. They wept over and stabbed them in the same moment, taking comfort, however, that this work was not to be performed by their enemies. Those who had been the principal agents in this slaughter, penetrated as they were with grief for the necessity, resolved not to survive those they had slain, and immediately collecting all their effects together, they set them on fire. This being done they cast lots for the selection of the men out of their number to destroy the rest. The last surviving man, after the nine had been slain by him, threw himself on his sword, but not until he had first set fire to the palace.

On the dawn of the following morning the Romans prepared for attack. But they were astonished in the highest degree on not hearing any noise but the crackling of the flames. They gave a loud shout in expectation of receiving an answer. Two women, who did not accept Eleazar's plan, along with five small children, hid themselves in a cistern during the slaughter. This noise alarmed the women in their place of retreat, who immediately coming out related the truth to the Romans as it really happened.

Far, however, from exulting in the triumph of joy that might have been expected from enemies, they united to admire the steady virtue and dignity of mind with which such numbers had been bound in one solemn compact.

This story, as related by the surviving women and the Roman soldiers, was recorded by Josephus, a man who hated the zealots and wished to find favor in the eyes of the Romans. All his writings have a strong pro-Roman flavor. But in describing the Masada story he could not help but admire the fortitude and strength of character in the Masada victims, so different to his own way of thinking.

For nearly two thousand years Josephus' story of Masada has been read, translated and puzzled over. Was it really true? Then in 1963 Professor Yadin led a mammoth expedition in the excavation of that famous place. Thousands of volunteers from all over the world joined many archaeologists to find out what was truth or fiction. Josephus was proved accurate in detail and the story of Masada came alive in our time. Modern Israelis wept when, in their digging, they came upon the charred remains of a child's sandal, a woman's coin purse, or when they found some securely-buried Scripture scrolls.

Yadin told in a lecture which Betty attended that the first scroll unearthed was a badly-gnawed parchment with writing from the book of Ezekiel. The part that could be easily read and was better preserved than others contained excerpts from chapter 37. Strong, down-to-earth scientists like Yadin could not help but shed tender tears when the first words they identified in that ancient scroll were: "Shall these bones live again?"

The main excavations were completed in 1965. Israel declared the rock of Masada a national monument. Every Israeli youth, fifteen years old, climbs Masada and spends the night on top amidst the historic remains of his heroic past. Every member of the Israeli defense forces is sworn in on the top of the mount.

Every ceremony for soldiers or youth alike ends with the same ritual. They face the city of Jerusalem while the story of the zealots is retold and they swear: "We shall remain free men!"

Then three times they shout: "Masada shall not fall again! Masada shall not fall again! Masada shall not fall again!"

The story of Masada is the key to understanding the Jewish spirit of today. The same spirit which defied a world of enemies and the overpowering strength of Rome two thousand years ago, has created the new young nation of Israel. For the last thirty years the Jews have gathered from all over the world to build their nation. At first the world sneered and then we marveled. As Mr. Begin wrote in his book:

It was the general opinion in the world that Jews preferred business to manual work. They would not be willing to leave their shops and offices for the hardships of life in the waste lands

131

*of Palestine with its bare hills and stony soil. Apart
from a handful of idealists and a few paupers, the
mass of Jews would stay where they were. . . . The
Jews might be good merchants, but soldiers, fighters? . . . The Jews had not handled arms for
thousands of years. Those not yet in Palestine
would be easily frightened off, and those already
there would have to look to the British for protection.*

Even the enemies of modern Israel must, just like
Josephus, admire and admit that the Jews have something many others would like to have: a spirit of
courage and a sense of destiny. Coupled with an Old
Testament heritage and the promises of God they have
proved something: they came here to stay!

February 4—
Saturday Evening

What a long long ride and over-tiring day! We
finally landed our weary bones in a kibbutz near the
Lebanon border, not far from the Good Fence.

We left Jerusalem early this morning. I didn't want
to leave. I always feel the need to linger a bit longer
and go once more to my two favorite spots—the
Garden Tomb and the hill of Calvary.

The bus did take our group for a second time to the
Tomb yesterday. We gathered there in the late afternoon after we returned from Masada. We felt the need

The Garden Tomb

Skull Hill
(Gordon's
Calvary)

to celebrate the Lord's Supper in the Garden before we left the city. Robert read the Scriptures and served the bread and wine to us. I sang a spiritual: "Were You There When They Crucified My Lord?" I turned toward Calvary as I sang the first verse. I turned toward the Tomb when I sang the second verse: "Were you there when they laid Him in the tomb?"

I looked at the simple garden tomb, hewn into the living rock and suddenly I saw it all again: a few men carrying a limp body down Calvary's hill to the new, unfinished grave of a well-to-do Jewish businessman, His brow overcrusted with blood, His side opened by a Roman spear, His hands and feet pierced and torn around the ugly nail wounds. Several crying women were wrapping Him hurriedly with some white linen strips while applying ointments and herbs to the lifeless form. Then quickly they laid Him in the tomb, for the sun was setting.

We had to finish our service in a hurry, too. The Garden would close the gates by sunset, also.

Just before we filed out to return to the bus, I whispered to Betty, "Let's take one more look at Calvary."

We walked around the garden without a word, up to the little high point that opens the view to Skull Hill, which some believe to be Calvary. I believe it, too. The last rays of the fast-setting sun bathed the rocks in warm gold and caused sharp shadows. I had never seen the "skull" design of the hill clearer. It was all there. The caves which form the dark eye holes, the rim of a nose, the shadows of a mouth—only the three crosses were missing.

One guide had told us that at Christ's time, below

the hill, there had been a field where people were stoned to death. So, this had been a place of many executions and much punishment.

Evening shadows lingered in an unearthly quietness turned reluctantly to leave. We walked for a last look past the opening in the cliff where He laid—and rose. "Were you there when He rose up from the grave?"

The bus drove us through the new city to our hotel. Betty and I sat without a word. I sometimes wonder if people around me think of me as unsociable because I withdraw occasionally into a silent shell. At times I cannot talk. Coming from my Lord's tomb is one of those times. I even find myself astonished that others *can* chat about everyday happenings after they walk away from such sacred moments. I always feel shaken to the depths of my soul when I visit that place in Jerusalem. This time it shook me deeper than ever. For the last two weeks I had been permitted to see many famous graves and monuments—all over Egypt, in Petra, and on Mount Nebo where Moses met his Lord and died after he had seen the land of promise—the story of death in various forms. But the Garden Tomb by the old city of Jerusalem does not speak of death. To me it is the triumphant story of life and victory over death.

What makes this tomb so different from the other exquisite burial places? I know that my Master's tomb is empty! Death could not keep Him and neither could His enemies! He was a King—the King of the universe! But He never built Himself an earthly palace nor did He prepare Himself a royal burial place. He never owned any slaves who would immortalize His name by giving their wretched lives to carve out a resting place for a dried-up mummy. He did not believe in slavery, but freedom for everyone.

They laid Him in a small borrowed grave which was not finished. It never got finished—ever. Even today one can see the unfinished part of a family tomb, but the family never used it! The inner walls are plain; no pictures, no writing to tell future generations the story and fame of the One who used it. The ceiling has no sun disks or stars to lighten up the darkness of death. The key of life is not engraved into the roughly-hewn rock anywhere. It's just a simple, empty grave. And the stone that closed the opening is gone, only the trough where it stood is left to be seen. Even though no hieroglyphs preserve the memory of the past, the empty stones seem to shout it out—and they shout and ring with joy.

I know now why Egypt depresses me and Jerusalem makes me sing. Egypt is the place where man *thought* that death was vanquished. Jerusalem is the place where death was conquered—forever! When the stone was rolled away—and the big stone was put there not to keep robbers out but to keep a broken body *in*—Christ rose as victor over death. His hands held no visible key of life. But the nail marks in His hands *are* the keys to everlasting life.

His story, never engraved into living rock, has lived in the hearts of freed men from generation to generation, up to our time. The walls of Egypt's tombs contain "the book of the dead." We have from God the Word of Life, the Bible. From it we know that He walked out of His tomb and He knew He would do so, for He knew who He was. "I am the way, the truth, and the life" (John 14:6), He said. He never *thought* that

He might vanquish death, He never *hoped* it could be so, He did it! He was God and He lowered Himself by His choice into the role of a slave and died as a cursed man. His body rested over the Sabbath quietly in darkness while His followers mourned and wept. He rose like the rising sun on the third day—and death had lost its sting and power forever.

This morning I sang again. The bus took the group to the Upper Room. Christians believe it to be where the Last Supper took place and where the Holy Spirit descended on Pentecost. We arrived too early and the place was still locked. So we had a short memorial service in the alley below. Robert read some words from the New Testament. He nodded at me and I sang my favorite song, "The Holy City."

I have sung that song hundreds of times since I came to America. I never dreamed that God would let me sing it some day while actually standing on the cobblestones of a narrow winding street in the old city of Jerusalem. The morning sun threw bright warm sunbeams into my face and I felt so happy and jubilant when I came to the last part of the song: "Jerusalem, Jerusalem, sing for the night is o'er. Hosanna in the highest, hosanna forever more."

Oh, how I long for Jerusalem to come to the end of the night! No other place has seen more heartache and human suffering! Not only did my Lord suffer and die here but the Jewish nation has a history of endless agony and terrible bloodshed.

It is hard to believe that some of those who call themselves followers of the crucified and risen Christ can be so harsh and judgmental when speaking about the Jews and their suffering. I still remember the time when an old preacher visited our small cottage while I was still a child. "The Jews deserved the destruction of Jerusalem and all the persecutions they had," he said with authority. "They brought it upon themselves because they rejected Christ."

Strangely enough the Nazis said the same things to us when they taught me as a teenager that the Jews were a condemned race. If ungodly men say such a thing, one knows the source of such hate. When Christians stand up in judgmental superiority and show no compassion, they deny the One whose name they carry. Christ loved Jerusalem so much that He wept over it. He *loved* His people, and He always will. They have special promises and Jerusalem has a prophetic future—and so does all of Israel.

How can one hear the story of Masada and say, "They deserved it?" How can anyone visit this land and not admire what three million Jews are doing right now for the land we Christians call the Holy Land?

We drove for a whole day through Israel to the north and my heart overflowed. I never saw the land with my own eyes before it became the state of Israel, but we have books in our library that tell about it and show pictures. For long centuries the land was mostly a dry treeless desert where Bedouins roamed. In the Jordan Valley some land was cultivated to feed its sparse population.

Long before Israel established itself, after the turn of the century, small groups of Jews returned to their forefathers' land because they longed for a home. The Arabs sold them "useless" land, bone-dry desert, mosquito-infested swamps, steep mountain terrain which could not be cultivated to raise food. One family could not even begin to struggle with such insurmountable odds—but several families could.

Out of the difficulties and the day-by-day need for protection in a hostile environment, the idea of the kibbutz was born. Today one cannot think of Israel without thinking of the many kibbutzim the land has, and more are in the making. The first kibbutz was started in 1910 and was named *Degania* after the blue cornflowers that grow in the nearby hills. A kibbutz is a communal way of life where everything is shared— the work, the food, the money, the joy and the cares. Individuals own nothing. All the profit goes into a common treasury and the families draw from it for special needs and wants. These Jewish kibbutz communities have done impossible and great things for their land. They drained big swamps and made them into the most fertile regions of Israel. They pumped water into the desert to irrigate and made it into immense flower and vegetable gardens. They removed thousands of rocks and improved the soil, terraced steep hills and planted trees. The land is changing from year to year and Israel is becoming more and more green and alive and full of people.

In the last twenty-five years Israel has planted 132 million trees and, slowly but surely, Israel's weather is improving. Forests affect the moisture content of an area, and now the rains are returning more frequently to the parched desert lands of Israel.

A new irrigation system developed in Israel is starting to be adopted in other parts of the world. Since water is so valuable in Israel, they have tried not to lose any of it by evaporation or flooding. So their irrigation system does not spray the water across the fields but trickles it into the ground, one drop at a time. Small amounts go a long way to keep the soil moist. Plastic covers create row after row of miniature hothouses in the desert, preserving life-giving moisture while the desert sun shines in.

Almost every house in Jewish territory carries also a solar heater on its flat roof. "It's the only thing we don't have to pay for so far," our guide said in a dry humor the time I visited Israel before. "We have plenty of hot water warmed by the sun, and solar energy is free." The Jews have a special talent to make both simple things and complex science work for their benefit.

That was true also in Germany, but I see Israel succeed where Nazi Germany failed. The reason my mind compares so often is because so many things I observe are so similar to the way I was once taught. The Germans tried to improve their land too—and they did. But everything Hitler built up and improved ended up destroyed by war in spite of the advanced scientific know-how. I know now that a nation is like a house and "unless the Lord builds the house, they labor in vain who build it" (Psalm 127:1). As long as Israel acknowledges the sovereignty of God, and her leaders confess their dependence and faith in the God of their fathers, God will honor them and their land will live. That is true for *any* nation, be it Egypt, Germany, Britain, Israel, or the United States of America.

Sometimes I wonder if America is slowly forgetting what young Israel is just beginning to learn. The same guide who talked about the free solar energy said it so simply to me, "We Jews *know* that God is our only

140

hope. We all know the Bible well and the history of our people. As long as Israel obeyed God they prospered. Whenever they followed other gods, the land and the people suffered. We want to do it *right* this time. The Book (the Old Testament) is taught in every Jewish school to every Jewish child and new-coming immigrant. We must never forget God again. If we do we will lose everything we have gained so far."

How true and how beautiful these words are!

I know something in my heart. If I did not have the privilege of living in America, I would want to live in Israel. It's the only other place I could feel at home. Maybe I'd even try kibbutz living. I think I could like it!

February 5—Sunday Evening

Today Samuel drove us to the Good Fence and up to the Golan Heights. Then we went back down to the Sea of Galilee.

Samuel and I have become good friends. Since he came from Poland and I from Czechoslovakia we feel we have a common root and we seem to understand each other. He caters a bit to my wishes and requests, and he answers patiently my many questions, bless his heart.

Last night we would have arrived earlier at our destination if I had not mentioned that I love cheese blintzes. Samuel took the whole busload of people to a kibbutz which makes the best blintzes in Israel, so I could taste them.

The Jews of different lands brought the customs and recipes of those lands with them to Israel. Cheese blintzes is a dish of Eastern Europe. I am afraid that my American fellow travelers couldn't quite follow my enthusiasm about the dish. For them apple pie with ice cream would make them feel at home.

I cannot help but marvel how Israel has managed to melt the Jews of so many nations together into a harmonious society. In the beginning they did not even have a common language. Most European Jews spoke Yiddish but many immigrants spoke only English, French, Spanish or some other language.

Israel decided to do the historically impossible. They decided to resurrect a dead language and make it their official language. They chose the Hebrew of the Old Testament. One lone Israeli professor was asked to design new Hebrew words for modern words and phrases that could be added to the ancient language. The Old Testament has no symbols for car, airplane, telephone—for example—because they didn't exist then.

Hebrew was taught to every Jew who entered the land or was born in it. The project was so successful and the pure form of the language so well preserved that Jewish schoolchildren can read fluently the ancient words on the Dead Sea scrolls in the Shrine of the Book museum. I watched them do it.

This revival of a dead language especially interested me because I once watched Nazi Germany try to do a similar thing. Hitler was so determined to develop a super race with a Germanic language that we young people in Nazi schools were not allowed to use any words with a Roman, French or other non-Germanic root. New words were created to replace the commonly-used ones. The project shattered with the end of the Third Reich.

Hebrew has become an officially recognized language again in Israel and is obviously here to stay. Most Jews speak more than one language. Their schools require the knowledge of Arabic and English. Many also speak German.

The rift between the Germans and the Jews is slowly healing. I saw many German and Austrian tourists in Israel and I feel good about it. It is my own deep conviction that West Germany had such a miraculous economic recovery because their government was willing to help Israel with reparation money. Nothing can ever repay the agony and the losses of human lives, but the stability of the West German mark helped to give the young state of Israel a solid foundation. The communist half of Germany has never helped Israel and I am convinced that it is their loss!

Israel, I found out this morning, is not only on the receiving end. They have begun to help others. The last time I was here the Good Fence didn't exist. But now Israel has become the big brother to the Christians in Lebanon.

The border between Lebanon and Israel had been closed since 1948. Less than two years ago, terrorists, whose aim is to destroy the Christian government in Lebanon and who also hate the Jews, crossed over the borderline and attacked a Jewish elementary school in Israel. They killed Jewish children and Israel wept. Israel loves its youth. They are the hope and strength of Israel's future. To help the children of Lebanon they opened one gate in the closed border. A Christian

143

The
Good
Fence
and
Hansi
at the
Lebanon
border.

Arab may come over on the designated spot and ask for food and medical help for himself and his children. "We know how it feels to watch children die," the Jews announced. "Bring them to us, we will help!"

The place was soon known as the Good Fence and while we stood there this morning behind sandbags and barbed wire, we watched Lebanese Arabs cross back and forth. Many come over now to work in Israel and their earnings keep whole families alive.

"Of course," Samuel grinned at me, "Israel isn't quite as unselfish in it as we say. It is wise politically to strengthen the Christian forces in Lebanon. If the terrorists take over, the Israeli people in the border areas are in grave danger. Nevertheless, we *do* want to help those who struggle to stay free. We Jews *know* how it feels to be oppressed!"

Yes, they know well and have not forgotten. Samuel told me many stories about the time when the Jewish underground forces fought the British. Samuel was Begin's driver during that time and through him I found out some details about the prime minister's younger years.

Begin was also born in Poland. His father died in a German concentration camp singing the Hebrew national anthem "Hatikvah." The word means "hope." Young Begin ended up in a Russian labor camp in Siberia because he was accused of being a spy for the British. When the Germans invaded Russia, he was set free. Even though he suffered inhuman cruelty, the imprisonment protected him from the ultimate tragedy of non-return which his family suffered. He *did* return to Eretz Israel. His father had dreamed of going there to his very last breath. Young Begin ended up

145

leading the patriotic Jews in their struggle for independence and freedom.

"I learned English from the British movies," Samuel smiled. "I never missed any. Once I was warned not to attend a certain movie because the English knew that I would come and they were eager to catch me. They had offered one thousand pounds for my head—dead or alive.

"I went anyway but did not stay to the end. They never caught me. After that my friends called me *Kehragh;* it means ice. They thought I had icy nerves."

I looked at Samuel. It was hard to picture him an icy underground fighter. He appeared so jovial, friendly and humane and his pleasingly-plump middle loved to chuckle. However, he did turn very serious when we drove past the Golan Heights. We didn't stop there this time, we did so at my last visit. I never understood why Israel was so unwilling to give up the Golan Heights after they had conquered it. Why argue about two or three miles of rocky land? It makes sense *only* after a person *sees* it. As long as the enemy controls the tops of the Heights, the Israeli valleys below are in easy shooting range of any hostile group.

The Jews lived life that way for two decades and their children had never slept in any other place but air shelters. Every night of their lives—and part of their days too, were spent underground.

During the Six-Day War in 1967 the hills were conquered in twenty-seven bloody hours, just before the United Nations declared a cease-fire to save Egypt, Jordan and Syria from being overrun by Israeli troops. Israel knew that they would be stopped within hours, but they *had* to get to the Golan Heights to secure a

146

normal life for the kibbutzim and other Jewish settlements below.

The Israeli tanks had returned from Sinai and come up from Jerusalem to fight the Syrians who had broken their own cease-fire and attacked several Jewish kibbutzim in the valley. The Jews knew that time was against them. They had to get up the hills before the UN stopped them. So they didn't wait for the cover of night but stormed the steep cliffs and heights at high noon. The tanks were low on fuel but who had time to wait for refueling? The kibbutzim brought in their trucks, tractors, ice cream trucks and bulldozers. These little unprotected vehicles helped and pushed the tanks up the steep hills. Tank after tank exploded, truck after truck blew up and the soldiers died by the hundreds. Out of one whole company only eight men made it to the firing trench of the enemy. Samuel fought on the Golan Heights, too.

There was not one little smile left in his eyes when he pointed to the Heights and said, "Little one, there is much of our best Jewish blood that soaked those hills. We lost more soldiers there than anywhere else. Many a mother is crying even today. Many wives lost their husbands, and children have no fathers because so many had to give their lives to secure the valley's peace and safety. How can we give up what cost us so much only to return to the old air shelters?"

I turned to Samuel, fighting tears. "I understand," I said. "But why are you holding so tight to Sinai? Do you need more land?"

He shook his head. "We don't need the soil of Sinai, we have enough to develop and cultivate right here in our land for hundreds of years. The Sinai desert is another strategic place which protects our shipping to the Eastern world. It's the only entrance to our single port of Eilat. Remember, the Six-Day War started because Egypt closed the entrances to our port. We had conquered Sinai twice, in 1948 and 1956. Each time we gave it back because the UN demanded it and we wanted peace. After 1956, UN troops took over the control of Sharm-el-Sheik and promised to secure the shipping rights of the gulf for us and Jordan.

"In May of 1967 Nasser told the UN troops to leave, so they left. He immediately brought in his troops and closed the three-mile wide Strait of Tiran again. Since Egypt does not permit us to use the Suez Canal we have no other shipping route but through the gulf or we must go around Africa.

"Israel protested and asked the UN for help, but we got nothing but talk and some lame promises—no action whatsoever. So we had to go and fight. Now we have fought for it three times. Would it not be stupid to give it back again or to trust their promises? The UN doesn't keep their word and Sadat can promise today, and tomorrow his successor can break the agreement. Egypt is not a democracy, they can have a revolution any time and nobody knows who will rule the next day. We have learned the hard way not to trust words any more. Remember, we have only three million Jews in our land. Whenever we lose *hundreds* of soldiers, it would amount to *millions* in your American proportion. How would you feel if you had lost several millions of American youth in Vietnam? Would you have given it up as easily as you did?"

I shook my head. No, I don't think so. To ask the Jews to give up what they so valiantly fought and died for would be the same as if Mexico would ask to have their land back which American settlers gained and won in the American-Mexican war. The fact will always remain that Texas, New Mexico, Arizona and parts of California are former Mexican territory. If it comes down to facts almost *all* of the United States is conquered, occupied land which was originally owned by someone other than the American settlers. The settlers won and today we have the United States of America. France, Poland, Russia and other European lands which won World War II and annexed large areas of Germany. The United Nations finds no fault with this so why is it that Israel wins war after war and the world demands their retreat every time?

I turned to Betty. "Tell me once more how Israel used the Bible in the 1948 and 1956 wars to conquer Sinai," I asked. Every time I hear her tell it or read about it, I see the hand of the living God in it.

It was dear Professor Yadin who later led the excavations of Masada who used his great knowledge of ancient and biblical history to lead Israel to victory every time.

"We had a terrible time with the Egyptians," Yadin tells in a book. "They held most of the Negev [desert] thanks to their control of the two main roads in the area: the Via Maris along the coast and the road that led across the Sinai sand dunes to a spot called Ahuja al Fahir, just behind the modern Egyptian encampment south of Beersheba."

Engineers and archaeology students went out at night with long poles and other equipment to find the hidden ancient road under the sand dunes. They found it and the sand was leveled off or planks were laid so that a motorized brigade with some ancient half-tracks could negotiate over it.

Before dawn they arrived behind the Egyptian fighting lines and took the place by complete surprise. The commanding Egyptian colonel was captured in his pajamas. "Where in the world did you come from?" was all he could ask.

The Egyptians and all of us do well to remember where the Jews come from. The Jews themselves must never forget it either. They are the people of the Book. And as long as they trust the God who inspired the writings of the Holy Word, they will be on the winning side. If they ever trust their military power and human strategy alone they will end up defeated.

I pray that America will remember it too. For the last two hundred years our land has been "one nation under God." If we ever feel we can proudly trust our strong military power and human wisdom alone, we shall go under.

May God protect us all!

February 6—Monday Evening

Tomorrow morning we have to rise before dawn to leave for the airport. Security checks will take a long time again and the suitcases are fuller than ever. Things we bought in Arab territory, like Bethlehem or Hebron, will be checked with closest attention. Tourists are also asked if any strangers have given them anything to take along to the States for a gift. The

Israelis have learned the hard way not to take *anything* for granted.

Our days in Israel were special days for me, they always are. God seems very real when I walk where once my Jesus walked. The weather was perfect, the land green and in bloom and the people everywhere so friendly. I am glad to go home to America again but what happy days we had!

Sometimes I wonder if tourists in Israel can enjoy this land to the fullest since we receive only the benefits but do not carry the daily burdens of this little harassed land.

I cannot forget what Prime Minister Begin said when he thanked Pastor Smith for his gracious words just before he walked off the platform: "We have very few good days in life. This *is* one of the few very good days of my life. I thank you from the bottom of my heart."

What a precious man he is. He is a deeply religious Jew who takes his faith in God and the Bible most seriously. I was told that he observes his Sabbath faithfully and worships regularly in his synagogue. He spends much time in prayer. I can see why. He carries great burdens. Israel is a democracy and he has at least nine major parties to contend with. To get them all to pull together must often be as impossible as when our American president tries to get our whole government under one hat. Democracy is the best form of government but not the easiest to handle. A dictator has a much easier time of it. Israel is the only true democracy in the Middle East with a continuing government where the parliament, not *one* man, makes the decisions. So, a change in leadership does not mean a change in government policy like it does in lands like Egypt or Jordan.

I shall continue to pray for Begin and also for Sadat. If Sadat means what he says and truly *wants* to make peace with Israel, his life is in great danger and only God can protect him. Some terrorist will try to remove him to stop the peace talks. If the next Egyptian leader is again pro-Russian it would close the door to future peace negotiations. No wonder the Bible tells us to pray for the peace of Jerusalem (see Psalm 122:6). It's the *only* place the Bible ever tells us to pray for. Peace in Jerusalem means peace for the world.

Two events of the last days have engraved themselves into my heart and memory. One happened while we were at the Sea of Galilee, yesterday. I love to be in Galilee because so many places tell about the life and work of Jesus. We stopped in Capernaum to see the ruins of a synagogue from just after Christ's time. From there a boat was supposed to bring us across the lake to Tiberias where we were to eat lunch.

To our great disappointment—and Betty's great delight—the Sea of Galilee was tossed by a strong wind and no boat dared to go out on the water. Betty had wanted to see a storm on Galilee every time she has visited before, but it had never happened. This time it did! The calm waters formed deep angry waves and whitecaps glistened in the bright sunshine. There was not one cloud in the blue sky but winds whipped the water into a frenzy. The winds seemed to come from nowhere.

The bus drove us around the lake to the shores of Tiberias and we ate the traditional "Peter's fish" in a restaurant beside the sea. Afterwards Betty and I stood

Ruins of the synagogue at Capernaum.

Storm on the Sea of Galilee.

and watched the waves spray high against the stone walls of the outer yard. In my inner eyes I saw a little fishing boat out there in the middle of the storm-tossed waters and I heard the disciples say, "Teacher, do You not care that we are perishing?" (Mark 4:38).

David our guide came and stood beside us.

Betty said to him, "Did you *know* that we would not be able to come across the lake by boat this forenoon? Was the storm predicted?"

David smiled. "No," he said, "we did not know that a storm would stop you from coming across by boat. We had made all the arrangements for your group to do so. These winds can come very suddenly and cannot always be anticipated. We don't know when the storms come, but we know one thing—when the winds blow from the east, no boat will dare to go out. The east winds bring the storm!"

"The east winds bring the storm," I thought. "Lord, is this a symbol of greater things to come? Will the strifes of the Middle East cause the next storm of war among the nations?"

The next unforgettable event happened today while we drove from the border of Lebanon on a newly-built Israeli road to Tel Aviv to prepare for our departure in the morning.

On our way we stopped at several places to sight see and shop some more. In the Valley of Jezreel we went to the tell of Megiddo. A tell is an artificial mound formed by layers of ancient cities. Some of them have been excavated. Megiddo is one of them. We know that the place existed in Old Testament times and during the Crusades, one of the most strategic points for the land of Israel.

To the Christians the area is known as the Valley of Armageddon. The valley is the only valley that runs east and west and any enemy of Israel had to come that way to attack them. The rest of the land is fortified by hills and mountains running north and south. This kind of land is easily defended.

No other place in ancient history had more battles fought over it than the city of Megiddo. The city was destroyed and rebuilt many times. As long as Israel was able to hold that fort, central Israel was safe. The enemy had to pass through that stronghold to enter the land of the Israelites.

Even today that valley is of great strategic value. It has become one of Israel's most fertile areas, since the swamps have been drained, and the land looks lush, green and fruitful. Geographically it is still the great crossing point for the nations of the north, south, east and west. In *any* war of the Middle East where Israel would be invaded, the enemy would have to come in through that valley.

The last Israeli wars brought no invaders to their land. The Jews conquered their enemy's land. But should anyone try to conquer Israeli territory, especially from the north (Russia) the valley of Armageddon could easily become the place of battle.

It is a known fact that modern Middle East wars are fought by airplanes and tanks. The small countries don't have the millions of manpower which the superpowers have. America, Russia, China and other big lands have greater human resources. Should a third world war ever begin on the soil of the Middle East, the Valley of Armageddon would become again the center of attention.

I stood on the hill of Megiddo and thought of the words of Revelation written by John, the beloved disciple of Jesus, our Lord: "And they gathered them together to the place which in Hebrew is called Armageddon" (see Revelation 16:16); "And I saw the beast and the kings of the earth and their armies assembled to make war against Him who sat upon the horse, and against His army" (Revelation 19:19).

It is hard to picture the peaceful green valley I looked at today filled with bloodshed and turmoil again. Will hate and war *never* end? Will mankind ever learn to live in peace with each other? Will Israel *ever* be able to trust her neighbors? For how long will Egyptian peasants find enough soil to grow food and what will happen when they run out?

The prophet Jeremiah said: " 'Peace, peace,' but there is no peace" (Jeremiah 6:14). " 'All is well,' but there is no peace" (Jeremiah 8:11).

I cannot help but think of another text in the New Testament which seems to fit the political tensions of our present time: "While they are saying, 'Peace and safety!' then destruction will come upon them suddenly" (1 Thessalonians 5:3).

As we stopped for lunch today at a kibbutz, I looked through the book rack and found a Jewish book in the English language. It is called, *My Shalom, My Peace* (Tel Aviv: Sabra Books), and it contains paintings and poems by Jewish and Arab children. Samuel smiled when he watched me buy that book.

He walked over to me and said, "Mr. Begin gave this book to President Sadat when he visited us in Jerusalem!"

Well, I hope Sadat reads it. I know that Begin has.

156

He read one of the poems to us in his speech on Wednesday night.

Betty and I have been reading in the book off and on, whenever we find a minute through the afternoon and evening. I cannot read too much at one time. These children's poems just get to me. I sit and weep.

Tonight I read another one. This one by Tami Ha Elyon, age 9½ from Tel Aviv:

Peace Is Good

When Peace will come, come indeed,
When the dream will finally be true,
When Messiah will come riding
*   on his great white steed,*
Solid gold through and through
And in his hand a banner hold
To show that our expectations
*   have taken place—*
Then husband and son, and father old
Need no more danger face
And a little girl will not ask
*   her mother anymore,*
"But Mommy, who needs war?"
Then in the shops they'll sell
Building blocks and every sort of animal,
While in town and village, little boys
Will no more know of guns for toys,
And person to person will smile instead
For Peace is good: I bet you lots!
No more wounded, no more dead,
No more shelters, no more shots,
And where once there was only
*   the bitter sigh,*
You will hear singing with spirits high.

Yes, little Tami, we both know that the Messiah will come. All we can do is to pray that He will come soon. There will be no peace on earth until He arrives. But when He comes then peace will reign forever. We both wait for that day with eager hearts, don't we?

For behold, I create new heavens and a new earth;
And the former things shall not be remembered or
  come to mind.
But be glad and rejoice forever in what I create;
For behold, I create Jerusalem for rejoicing,
And her people for gladness.
I will also rejoice in Jerusalem, and be glad in My
  people;
And there will no longer be heard in her
The voice of weeping and the sound of crying.
No longer will there be in it an infant who lives but
  a few days,
Or an old man who does not live out his days;
For the youth will die at the age of one hundred
And the one who does not reach the age of one
  hundred
Shall be thought accursed.
And they shall build houses and inhabit them;
They shall also plant vineyards and eat their fruit.
They shall not build, and another inhabit,
They shall not plant, and another eat;
For as the lifetime of a tree, so shall be the days of
  My people,
And My chosen ones shall wear out the work of
  their hands.
They shall not labor in vain,
Or bear children for calamity;

For they are the offspring of those blessed by the
  Lord,
And their descendents with them.
It will also come to pass that before they call, I will
  answer; and while they are still speaking I will
  hear. The wolf and the lamb shall graze to-
  gether, and the lion shall eat straw like the ox;
  and dust shall be the serpent's food. They shall
  do no evil or harm in all My holy mountain,
  says the Lord (Isaiah 65:17–25).